Lead, Follow or Get Out of the Way!
Volume One

Library of Congress Control Number: 2009920636

ISBN: 978-1-57833-436-0 (hard cover)
ISBN: 978-1-57833-440-7 (soft cover)
First Printing January, 2009

Printed by Everbest Printing Co., Ltd., Nansha, China through **Alaska Print Brokers.**
Book design: Vered R. Mares, **Todd Communications**
Cover photo: courtesy of Jon Little
This book was typeset in 12 point Times New Roman.

Published by

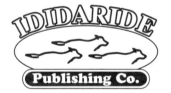

P.O. Box 735
Sterling, Alaska 99672
Tel. (907) 260-3139 • Fax (907) 260-3269
info@ididaride.com • www.ididaride.com

Distributed by:
Todd Communications
611 E. 12th Ave.
Anchorage, Alaska 99501-4603
(907) 274-8633 (TODD)
Fax: (907) 929-5550
with other offices in Ketchikan, Juneau, Fairbanks and Nome, Alaska
sales@toddcom.com • **WWW.ALASKABOOKSANDCALENDARS.COM**

Contents

Acknowledgements

Thanks to all my family members who succumbed to my demands for proof reading and feed-back on the book. Thanks to Dr. Denny Albert, DVM and Gary Paulson for making suggestions regarding content. I shall someday forgive them both, if not thank them for making me leave out some of my favorite parts. I know they appreciated the book's humor however, for they each said to me repeatedly, "You've got to be kidding!" Thanks to Doug Capra, my English teacher at Seward High School, for his noble efforts to teach me to write long ago and now for his editorial suggestions for the book.

Special thanks to my wife Janine for her help throughout this process but especially for feigning interest the many times she was unable to escape the rambling verbal recitations inflicted upon her as I probed the recesses of my alleged mind in search of actual content for a book.

Introduction

My love of sled dogs was born in 1963. I was four years old when my dad, Dan Seavey, took the plunge into sled dogs. I had the distinct privilege of running dogs through the great Alaskan wilderness for ten years before the Iditarod Trail Sled Dog Race was "invented." When that came along, I was a young teenager and served as my dad's handler for the first two Iditarod races in 1973 and 1974.

As I reflect on those experiences, I'm sure I am glamorizing it in my mind. How much does a young kid care about the wilderness and beautiful scenery anyway? To be sure, the enthusiasm of my father had a lot to do with my "loving" dog mushing. I do know winter gear for kids in those days was actually nonexistent, so anything warm in women's size small was rolled up, tucked in, and pressed into service. Footwear was leather bottomed Air Force surplus mukluks with about as much traction as a wet bar of soap, in some size large enough so the toes worked best folded over the top like elf shoes. Mitts were cold, wet, or so big I looked like I had a sheep skewered on each hand. I don't know how many miles I traveled with three or four

Introduction

dogs, following behind my dad's team in those days, but if valuable lessons and good memories are any indication, it must have been a million.

There were all those wonderful times I nearly froze my feet. And the time we got snowed in and walked 25 miles breaking trail in front of the teams. And the time I did multiple barrel rolls down the hard-drifted slope of a mountainside, sled and all. (I finished the stunt right-side up standing on the runners as if nothing had happened, albeit a few yards off the trail.) Oh yeah, and the time I went through the ice at 14 below and froze into a big Popsicle. There was the time the snow bent the brush over the trail on a 20-mile stretch, leaving a little tunnel just big enough for the dogs. We plowed through the entire 20 miles using our faces as trail grooming equipment. There was the one and only time I lost my team, but we won't go into that. I even had the distinct honor of getting stomped by a moose, all before I had a driver's license.

Once, as I followed my dad with my five-dog team, he attempted to run his larger team across a badly glaciated side hill. It was a place where a spring oozed out of the side of a mountain all winter and froze, creating what amounted to a giant ice chute sloping at about a 45-degree angle down the mountain. Dad's team hit the ice at a pretty good clip and made it about half way across before they spun out and lost traction. As they slowed down, the sled started sliding sideways down the ice. Dad got off and tried to pull the sled uphill to keep it from going down the chute, all the while coaxing the dogs to find just a little more traction to inch across the ice-covered incline.

They seemed to be making progress until Dad's feet slipped out from under him. As he slid down into the team, his boots became entangled in the towline just ahead of the sled. Helpless, he swung like a pendulum until his head was downhill, his boots still firmly snared in his towline.

His sled, now traveling in the same general downhill direction, ran over him going backwards.

There he lay, on his back, head downhill at a steep angle, feet caught in the towline, his sled straddling him. His team did their best to try to pull him and the sled across the glacier, but their best efforts were to no avail. Suddenly they lost traction altogether and the entire mess slid about 75 feet down the ice chute. Only a well-placed deadfall interrupted their descent, and prevented them from landing in Cook Inlet, at high tide.

"Well, don't just stand there laughing your fool head off, get me out from under this thing!"

My dad seemed to actually enjoy these adventures, and growing up with them, I thought they were just part of normal life. Even the most extreme or dangerous experiences were treated casually as though this were the sort of thing one expects here in Alaska. Misadventures were relished, ignored, or made into a joke.

Many of the misadventures I recall centered on the sled dogs, though Dad was also a commercial fisherman and a high school history teacher.

"Hey Dad, I think Kobuk has had enough of this bumpy road. He just puked out the back window of the jeep."

"Better'n pukin' in the jeep like last time."

"Yea, it was really cool. It went all over that car behind us, and I think the driver's window was even open."

"Well, I'll be darned, that looks like ol' Eckelson, the high school principal following us in his new car. Couldn't have happened to a nicer guy! Har, har, har! Way to go Kobuk! How about another ripe fish head when we get home?"

"Dad, he just puked again."

"Did he get Eckelson again?"

"Nope. It's inside this time."

"You can clean it up when we get home."

Introduction

"Nope."

"Then you're not riding in this jeep for a good long while, young man. You hear me?"

"Aw shucks, I guess I can't go to school then, right?"

"Wrong. You and your brother hook up those yearlings tomorrow and run them across the river to town. You two aren't missing school."

"Uh, the river is wide open, fifty feet wide, five feet deep!"

"You'll manage. Don't be late."

"Where will we tie up the dogs all day?"

"Ask Mr. Eckelson."

The fond memories of growing up with a yard full of sled dogs are just too many to recount. The chores to be done. Watering a yard full of dogs as a small boy with my Radio Flier "truck" and a two-gallon bucket full of water. Well, half full by the time I pulled that wagon out the bumpy driveway to the dogs. There was the joy of traveling with eight big dogs and a dog sled in a tiny Willy's Jeep. And those lovely items, consisting mostly of protein and hosting all manner of creepy-crawlies, waiting to be transformed into dog food in a wood fired contraption made of a steel 55-gallon drum.

"You boys don't forget to cook dog food today."

"Yeah, sure. We're on it, just as soon as that bear gets his fill of halibut heads and wanders off."

"There's a bear? You better not let him wander off. You better put him in the pot too, you hear me?"

"Dang it!" I said to my brother Darian, "Why did you have to tell him?"

"Cause, it's my turn to shoot and your turn to skin, that's why."

For several years, beginning in the '60s, before the first 1000-mile Iditarod Race, I had the honor of knowing the late Joe Redington Sr. His enthusiasm and influence on mushers is legendary. I recall conversations between Joe and my dad and Tom Johnson, my dad's commercial fishing partner, the three of them more or less day dreaming and brainstorming about some kind of long distance sled dog race. I was just a kid, but Joe's passion for dogs energized everyone he came in contact with, and the Seaveys were no different. My dad was particularly intrigued with the idea of an event where a guy could actually travel somewhere with dogs rather than just circling a groomed track and returning to the dog truck. A history teacher and romantic, he imagined himself traversing the great state of Alaska like the prospectors, trappers, and explorers of old.

Eventually the idea of a race from Anchorage to Nome emerged. The story of the birth of the Iditarod Race has been well chronicled, but what I remember most about the months preceding the first race was the big question. Is this even possible? When the racers eventually made it to Nome, my dad in an impressive third place, the important thing was not so much what place you came in, but the fact that you came in at all. The feeling has never left me and I guess it still influences my racing today. First and foremost we are privileged to travel with these wonderful animals through beautiful and awe-inspiring country. To finish is the goal. To win is a bonus.

Why was third place an impressive finish for my dad? Well, he was not a professional dog man or racer of any kind. He was a schoolteacher and recreational musher on his very first dog race. He beat some pretty good teams too. The key was he trained hard and learned everything he could, which was especially challenging since nobody knew, at that time, how to run a 1000-mile race. He studied historical accounts of long distance dog trips, paying special attention to dog care ideas. There were still a few old-timers around too, in the early 70's; sons of the dog team mail carriers out of Seward, our hometown. These

Introduction

guys were interviewed and gladly shared what they re-membered of the old days. Dad was an innovator, even though innovation in those days often meant dusting off some of the knowledge of a bygone era.

One:
Dog Smart

This book is meant to help you develop a long-distance dog team, and gain an understanding of dogs in general. It's not a "how to win the Iditarod" book. There is a serious lack of good information and a lack of sharing of the available information by those who have it. I want to fill in the gaps so people eager to run sled dogs and get ready to run the Iditarod and other races don't have to guess at everything. Beyond that is the realm of the ultra-competitive and I won't be going into that, at least not now.

I'm writing this for people who want to learn about sled dogs, but I also hope it will bear truth for anyone involved with working dogs. I write about the Iditarod because I think it's the ultimate race and the ultimate test of dogs and musher skill. Besides, long distance mushing is the only thing I know about where dogs are concerned. But I have a hunch that folks working with dogs in other capacities will nod and chuckle a time or two as they recognize their own champions between these covers, albeit not in harness. Shoot, even pet owners might pick up something of value here, but I hope they have a sense of humor!

Dog Smart

To my dismay, there has been a "sissification" of our sport over the last few years because of outside pressure and the general "pansifying" of our culture. A lot of mushers spend way too much time justifying themselves and the sport, talking about how good they are to their dogs, how happy their dogs are, etc. I'm not going to do that here. Let's just skip all of that and see if we can start to view Man's Best Friend from a little different perspective.

Let's look at how a dog thinks and reacts from a dog's point of view, not from a human point of view. Even some of the best dog people fall into the error of asking themselves "How would I feel if I were in that dog's position?" The problem is that you and the dog have entirely different viewpoints even when viewing the same thing.

The Pack

There is a vast difference between the mindset of a western civilized human, and a pack oriented canine. For example, we humans put a lot of store in being nice. The dog just wants us to be definite. We try to be fair. The dog just wants us to be consistent. We humans harbor a great fear of death, and our dogs are more fearful of the unknown. To help us cope with our fear of death humans adhere to belief systems. Take away the dog's fear of the unknown by eliminating uncertainty in his life and your methods and routines will become his belief system.

Dogs are pack animals, and this is obvious in a dog team setting. We mushers are privileged to participate in this ancient society. Dogs need the pack structure to be balanced and complete. The pack will form and you can participate at whatever level you wish. As a successful musher, you must take your place at the top of the pack, and provide structure and discipline for your dogs. You must remove uncertainty from their lives by providing strong, consistent, and reliable leadership.

No, really. Listen, besides food and water, and maybe a den to crawl into, this pack structure is just about the most important thing to a dog's overall well-being. Why? Well, I'm guessing it's because the pack-structured society is precisely how they secured food, water and shelter since ancient days and still would today without our help. The most able and dominant member is the pack leader. The pack follows the strong leader and travels extensively in search of life's necessities. Individuals lacking the pack instincts in days gone by almost certainly perished alone. Pack oriented dogs thrived, reproduced and passed on the strong pack instincts to future generations and the need for a pack leader persists throughout the generations. A dog must either follow a strong leader, or become one. Lead, follow or get out the way.

Determining the pack leader in ancient times was simple. It was pretty much about who could beat up whom, and I suppose tackling and killing a 1200-pound moose would look pretty good on the resume as well. This inherited pack dominance struggle often leads to some pretty rough and tumble behavior among our "little sweeties," but today we humans have quite an advantage in the auditions for pack leader if we choose to participate. We can, almost without effort from the dog's point of view, provide food, water, and shelter. Now all we have to do is act like a strong leader, provide structure and discipline, and remove uncertainty from the dog's life, and we can be a pack leader on steroids!

Here's the essence of it. The way I train dogs doesn't really involve a whole lot of training in a traditional sense. I simply insert myself into their life system as the "Big Dog" (I just can't bring myself to say "Alpha male" here). Then from there we work with their natural inclinations and build attitude and commitment, until I can absolutely depend on them to do what I need them to do. This is the philosophy of my training program.

Dog Smart

Throughout the following pages you will see glimpses of dogs as they really are. They aren't always nice to each other by our standards; though they can be very affectionate to humans they are comfortable with. They are honest and predictable though, true to their ancient life stream. And they are eternally loyal to their pack leader. You and I should be honored that these amazing animals would allow us to fill that role in their world.

Love your dogs enough to see to their every need and respect them enough to have high expectations of their abilities.

Sled Dog Mentality

Well, if you're going to run dogs, even in a semi-professional manner, you have a lot to learn. That's the beauty of competition. It forces you to do things right. Now, if your goal is to have a few mutts to go play in the snow, then all you need is mutts and snow, but if you're a beginner and you want to finish a 1000-mile race like the Iditarod, then you better get a leg up on the ol' learning curve.

If you're half observant, a quick look at the outfits leaving the starting line will tell you that there is a lot of diversity among Iditarod teams. There are different dogs, different sleds, different towlines and harness systems. And even the mushers are, well, different. Funny how the best teams finish so close together though, when their methods seem so far apart.

I suppose there are many different right ways to do things, and I'm not sure mine are the best, but it's what makes sense to me after more than 40 years with dogs. You see, good drivers have their own systems, born out of unique personalities, locations, dog genetics, and experiences. If you see an idea used by a good driver and think you might like to copy it, you better also look at all of the other things that will be affected and see if the idea fits with your setup. You may find that unless you copy a lot of what that driver is doing, copying one idea may be more of a problem than a help.

For example, a certain race-winning musher used to talk (and talk, and talk some more) about how he always ran his dogs full speed down hills in training. It built in speed and separated out the weak ones, he claimed. I can't say otherwise, 'cause this guy had a fast team, and the weaklings definitely weren't still in there when he passed me! Now, if you were inclined to try that particular method, you'd best have dogs designed for speed and have excellent training trails. Otherwise you would be far better off trotting down hills, at least in poor trail conditions. By the way, that musher has more than once been passed by trotting teams later in the race when the jets flamed out on that speedy team of his.

One thing most of us agree on though, whether we drive standing or sitting, use half harnesses or freight harnesses, use necklines or not, whether we train long and slow or short and fast, the most important part of the whole shebang is the quality of the dogs.

Most of the dogs we use in racing today are still descendents of Alaskan and Siberian (as in "from Siberia") native village-type dogs. These dogs are hardy survivors of the harshest elements and of necessity were culled by their ancient masters to only the individuals that would perform as needed. The main thing needed was "someone to pull this dang sled!" The dogs often ran loose, half wild, and hunted for their own food, an important part of their natural urge to travel.

In modern times different breeds have been mixed in over the years with varied results, but eventually quarter-crosses turn to eighths turn to sixteenths and then, who's counting? As Canadian sprint mushing great, Terry

Dog Smart

Streeper told me, "If its one-eighth pointer you have to at least give it credit for being seven-eighths husky."

I believe Alaskan Husky sled dogs are quite different than most purebred dogs you see in a breed book. They have been perfected by thousands of years of natural selection and survival of the fittest, while purebred dogs are selected mostly for their looks or for some other unique purpose. Huskies are much closer to their wild canine roots, and so respond to natural instincts more resembling those of their ancestors. "So what?" you say. "Let's get to the top-secret training tips, already!" Well, keep your mukluks on there because this may be the most important thing you ever learn about sled dogs.

Have you ever seen anything in the wild resembling a Dalmatian for example? No, not a zebra. I mean a canine. Nope? How about a Chihuahua? Didn't think so. A Daschund? These are all basically man-made genetic freaks. I have no idea how you train a Chihuahua, but if you look at northern-type wild canines, you can get some clues about your sled dogs.

The most important thing to remember is to think like a dog. No, not your grandmother's poodle! Think like a northern breed canine with a pack mentality, and a life-stream stretching back tens of thousands of years.

Thinking like a dog isn't natural for people. It takes time, because dogs are entirely different than we are. Dogs pretty much operate in the "now." They don't have plans for the future, and they don't have regrets or hold grudges from the past. They don't have jealousy or hatred. If another dog has something they want, well they want it too, but they don't wish anything bad for the other dog like a person might. And probably most importantly, dogs don't judge.

People are afflicted with the damnable need to decide upon everything we encounter, whether it is good or bad. Further, we think our judgment on the matter is the correct judgment no matter what. For a dog, however, there is no good or bad; a thing simply "is" and that is that. Sure, they recognize from experience when something pleasant or unpleasant is about to happen, and react accordingly, but the instant the situation passes, they have no opinion about it. They don't have the ability to decide whether that situation was fair or unfair, right or wrong, good or bad.

Typical sled dogs are much closer to their wild origins than the dogs most people are familiar with. That could be at the root of a lot of the misunderstandings folks have about dog mushing. They can't imagine their dog running a thousand-mile race. One look at their dog and I would probably have to agree with them! But beyond physical traits, the instincts of these sled dogs are fine tuned to the task at hand.

There are plenty of books around by folks who want to teach you how to potty train a puppy, or teach him to shake hands or paws or whatever. There are excellent trainers working with search and rescue dogs and such, but it's a different task and a different approach. Then there are a few folks who try to use pet training methods for sled dogs. Forget about it.

I am sure you will forgive my irreverent nature, and lack of sentimentality or etiquette. I have a lifetime of working and relating with a certain type of dogs, and I don't claim any expertise with other breeds. If you happen to know a lot about other types of dogs you may find that some of this information applies to your critter too, but I suspect that the more humans have had a hand in forming the breed you work with, the further they are from their natural instincts. I'm not sure what instincts are useful to some of the pampered pet dogs anyway, besides perhaps, not wetting the bed!

Pure-breed working dogs are a different matter. At least there was at one time some sort of performance standard attached to their meal ticket, and some of the functions of these breeds are easy to relate to the age-old instinct to run and catch and kill food. For example, the herding dogs I have had the pleasure of watching seemed to me to be only one muscle twitch away from accomplishing the task of their ancient forefathers. They did an excellent job of outrunning and rounding up the stock but someone taught them not to snack on the "silly wooly things" (or eliminated that instinctive trait through selective breeding). Same concept with retrievers, tracking dogs, guard dogs, hunting dogs, and others— parts of their ancient instincts are honed and parts are minimized or eliminated. Sadly, many genetic flaws are highlighted by hundreds of generations of inbreeding.

Now, I'm a brave guy, but I just got up and locked the door in case some pure breed "fancier" is looking in the window at this page. I'm sure if they knew a Barbarian like me was disrespecting their purebred, I'd be in hot water for sure! Oh well.

I have been asked many times by guests at our sled dog tour business, "How do you make these dogs go?" I politely tell the person that the dogs really want to go, just stand by and watch. That isn't even the whole story. You will see before I get done with you here that we aren't just looking for dogs that run along because we make them do it. We don't want dogs who are just willing to run. We aren't even looking for dogs who like to go. Our dogs run, and run, and run some more, because they simply can't help it. They have to run. They have inherited the urge to run and hunt for food. Nobody has to tell them. Thousands of years of instincts are raging just below the surface, and they must run.

The most important thing in racing is the quality of the dogs. Don't kid yourself. Some dogs are just better than others.

I'm writing this hoping to share some good information with beginning dog mushers, and I've got to tell you the truth: Not all sled dogs are good enough to run the Iditarod, the world's premier distance race, or compete at the top of any dog racing style for that matter. You may have 20 dogs in your yard already, and if you got them for cheap or free you likely need to start over. A free sled dog is often like free advice; it's worth what you paid for it. On the other hand if your goal is to finish the Iditarod for the first time, you don't need to buy last year's winning team, either. You wouldn't know what to do with it if you had it and your money is better spent elsewhere.

One thing I've learned over the years is that nearly everything involved with long distance racing is about balance. You have to find the balance in everything. Sleds should be light weight, but tough enough to hold up. Feed fat to your dogs when they are working, but not so much you upset their digestion. Run behind the sled but not so much that you are too tired to do your chores when you get to the checkpoint. Dogs have to be fast, but know how to slow down for the long haul. Get the idea? Everything has to be in balance.

Another way to say it is, as soon as you find something that works, start looking for its limitations. If you buy dogs, spend some money and get good ones, but if you are a beginner don't spend the family fortune and run out of dog food money.

I suppose you're itching to get started here so let me encourage you that in about two years you could be ready. This isn't a quick in and out deal. The first thing you're going to need is a dog team. You probably already knew that, but unless you have cared for (and paid for) a yard full of dogs in the past you don't really know what it means. Well, I'll leave the preaching to someone else (for now), but think about it before you take the plunge. It's a

Dog Smart

big undertaking and our sport doesn't need wannabes who aren't ready to make the commitment to dog care and the personal responsibility it requires.

Two:
Dog Acquisition

You can either buy a team or raise it yourself, depending upon how much money you have to put into it. Believe me, neither way is cheap. Buying adult dogs allows you to run them right away, and if you get good ones they can teach a new musher quite a bit. Raising your own can yield better results in the long run if you train them well; besides, you get the pick of every litter. I have bought a lot of dogs over the years and been mostly disappointed, but initially, if your goals are realistic, you can pick up some honest troops from other kennels. I think the best way is a combination approach. Get a few well-trained dogs to get you started, and raise the best pups you can.

Buying Dogs

Only buy dogs from mushers who are at least as good as you hope to be. A so-called drop out from a top team is still likely better than the star of a so-so team. My experience has proven this many times over. I have bought out kennels of fairly successful mushers or bought dogs straight off of their "A-team" thinking that at least some of these dogs must be pretty good. Wrong! Not a single dog in there could contribute to my team. Conversely, I have sold dogs that hadn't a prayer of making my team and actually heard back through the grapevine that the buyer doesn't think I'm much of a dog man because I was dumb enough to sell such a good dog. Well I'm glad he thinks so 'cause I sure don't want that dog back.

There are a lot of dogs for sale out there. I suppose every dog is for sale at some price, but obviously, the ones advertised for sale have been selected by their owner to no longer "be here." There are reasons why dogs are for sale. Some are good reasons like finances, or kennel space, or the neighbors, but still, the ones for sale are the ones the owner has chosen not to keep. Some of the sales pitches can range from heart-rending to comical, so let the buyer beware. One difficulty in buying dogs for a distance team is that until you spend days or weeks on the trail with a particular dog you really don't know how he will perform in a 1000-mile race. In fact, you won't really know until you actually run him in a 1000-mile race.

Buy dogs based upon what that dog has actually done, or can reasonably be expected to do.

If you are buying dogs to add experience and stability to a distance team and act as your core, they should have previously run at least a 300-mile race and finished in a position at least as high as your goal would be if you were to enter that race. They don't necessarily have to be Iditarod veterans, but they should have proven themselves in long races, at least 300 miles long. Youngsters and breedings should be out of dogs who have finished the Iditarod or whatever your ultimate race will be, in a position at least as high as you hope to finish.

"But this dog is the grand-daughter of a dog from a kennel that took third in the Snowball Classic 50-miler, four years ago!"

"Right, uh, did you say your neighbor was selling a dog?"

The best way is to know the reputation of the kennel selling you the dog. There are plenty of good dogs that top drivers realize won't quite make a winning team. These are still good athletes that can be pillars in a beginning team. Think about it. A good-sized championship kennel can afford to part with dogs that are better than the best ones in many other teams.

Sled dogs generally are ready to start harness training at about twelve months, can race as early as 18 months, and keep racing up to about ten years old. Don't buy old dogs and hope for one last miracle season. Get young or prime age dogs that will help you for a few years. Avoid "package deals" that include dogs you wouldn't otherwise buy. You are probably getting dumped on.

That's one of my big gripes with some kennels. A new guy comes along, just getting started, and they dump dogs on him that are not going to help him, dogs that will retard the development of his kennel, and may discourage the guy so bad he doesn't stick with it. Meanwhile, the new musher feeds these critters for a year or more before he even figures it out. It's even worse when they do it to junior mushers.

"This isn't much of a dog, but he will probably be good for a junior team."

That's the perfect way to discourage the future of our sport. Put a young musher on a long race with poor dogs, and tell them to go have fun. If anyone doesn't need to have worries about the performance of the dogs in the team it's a junior musher.

Now, if you are mostly interested in recreational mushing, you can have a ball with some great older dogs or some that aren't quite top-flight athletes. Not everyone wants to race. In fact probably the majority of teams aren't

Dog Acquisition

interested in any type of serious competition. Just make sure the dogs you acquire are suited to what you have in mind.

For my money, I want dogs that work all the time. Some drivers talk about a dog that is smart and knows how to rest while running. Well, there's a fine line between "smart" and lazy. Beware of terms like "inconsistent." I've put up with a few dogs that didn't run quite as smoothly as the rest of the team, or weren't quite as athletic, but one sure test is up a big hill. All eyes forward, all tug lines like guitar strings. No exceptions.

Another thing you can tell right away is the dog's disposition. I prefer dogs that are happy and friendly, but there are a lot of good dogs that are just more high-strung than that and seem to be timid, at least at first. You may not even be able to approach the dog right away, but if you are buying him, the present owner should be able to go up to the dog and handle him without reeling him in on the chain. If he can, you probably will be able to as well, given a little time.

You will probably want eight or more good dogs to run and form the core of your team while you raise your pups. You want at least one good leader in the bunch. And here's the key: Buy at least two good brood bitches, bred to the best stud you can manage. This is your future. Don't scrimp on this.

Good honest team dogs of competitive Iditarod caliber will cost you from $1500 to $3000 each. A good leader may be over $3000. If your breeding females are proven racers, already bred to a championship stud, you are getting a good deal if you buy them for $2000-2500 apiece. It's easy to spend double these figures, too. A breeding alone will cost at least $500 and a top stud will fetch $1000 per female bred. You can probably get a ten or fifteen percent discount on package deals if you buy several dogs.

Some people take great exception to paying these prices for a dog. Well, you don't have to, but you aren't likely to ever run with the top teams if you don't. And nobody is making a profit selling experienced race dogs at these prices. Considering the years of work, risk, and dedication it takes to produce top caliber racing dogs, the opportunity to buy them and shortcut the process is a good deal at almost any price.

These figures assume you want to develop a competitive team someday. If you "just want to finish" I suppose you could do it with lesser dogs, but for me, much of the joy of the sport is witnessing the performance of truly fine athletes and even when I am 90 years old and bringing up the rear, I plan to run the best possible athletes I can manage.

Shop around, compare prices, take your time, and see the dogs run. Then, take a deep breath and write the check.

By the way, don't get loaded up with too many females either. You only want to deal with so many coming into heat, and overall you can expect a little better performance from males. I'd certainly keep the ratio at least 50:50 or a little in favor of the males.

Breeding

This will by no means be a complete master's course on breeding sled dogs, but if you are going to be in it, there are some things you have to know. If you bought your two or more brood bitches from a kennel with a good reputation, a winning record, and a great genetic line of dogs (and if not, I can't imagine why not), then the best possible value is probably for you to get both of those females bred to the best stud in that kennel, suitable to the genetics of the females. In the heat of negotiating, or in the warm

Dog Acquisition

fuzzy afterglow of a dog deal, you may get a kennel owner to "throw in" the breedings at a discount, say half price. Soon you will have ten or twelve dogs, and a pretty good sampling of the best genetics of a winning kennel, for the price of two bred females. Well, plus food. Oh, and vet expenses. You may have just the teeniest expense in maintenance as well. And a lot of work too, I suppose. But other than that it's pretty cheap! (It will set you back about $500 per dog per year for basic maintenance, not counting labor.)

Now, if you are going to breed your females, you will have to decide whom to breed them to. I feel that the dogs to be bred have to be both outstanding individuals, and come from outstanding lines (genetic background or family tree). If possible you should breed dogs together in the same genetic lines, to preserve the desirable traits in the line. This is a fairly complicated subject, but here are a few ideas.

First, unless you bought females specifically with breeding in mind, the ones already hanging around your kennel may not be suitable for breeding at all. The ideal stud dog isn't likely in your kennel either. Maybe they are, but don't just breed whatever you happen to have and hope for the best. The outcome is not likely to produce dogs better than what you already have, and almost certainly will not yield a single champion. This is one of the harsh realities of this sport, and if one is honest, any competitive venture. The Bad News Bears only win in the movies. Sorry. No amount of wishing will overcome the facts. Trying harder or being more motivated will improve you compared to you, but it won't overcome a lack of physical and mental talent, especially if your competitors have all of the above.

Remember, for the sake of our discussion, the litter is going to get half its genes from each parent. Ignore

legends and wives tales that say the mother is all that matters or the father is the most important. In some litters
that may appear to be the outcome, but the pups are half
Mom, and half Dad. If one or both parents are losers, by
racing standards, you could still get the odd decent dog,
but mostly they will be losers too. By the same token,
if you breed two great individuals together, you are more
likely to get a better percentage of good dogs, but if either
or both parents are the exception rather than the rule in
their particular genetic line, then you are still likely to get
more disappointments than if you breed two top perform-
ers, both from great lines.

Breeding is sort of like Murphy's Law, so breed both
great lines and great individuals, and leave open fewer
possibilities that the breeding "can go wrong."

Now, breeding two great dogs from two different
great genetic lines can still yield dismal results. The problem here is that we breeders don't even really know what
it is that makes a great dog great, so what traits are we
breeding for? Sure, we have parameters about size, coat,
feet, conformation, etc., but it is well known that the most
important ingredients in a great sled dog are invisible. Is it
a larger-than-normal heart, oversized lungs, or some other
organ that makes the difference? Maybe the production
of some hormone or extra intelligence is the key. I have
a pretty good idea what makes the greatest distance dogs
stand head and shoulders above the rest, but we'll get into
that later. The point here is the physical traits that make
dogs in one line great, may be different than the outstanding traits in another line.

Line-breeding or breeding dogs of similar background together, often produces the best results because
it preserves the traits of a great line of dogs rather than
mixing or diluting those traits with those of another line.

Dog Acquisition

Suppose the dogs in the Muktuk line have a digestive tract with extra fast nutrient absorption, and always have extra energy on races. The Ugruk dogs have thicker tendons and ligaments and are never sore or tired, always finishing strong. You get to the finish line and the Muktuk female and the Ugruk male were your two best dogs. You breed them together with great expectations. Time passes and lo and behold you get only one out of six pups anywhere near as good as either parent on an off day.

How can that happen? Well, without going on and on about dominant and recessive genes and other stuff I probably don't really understand, let's just say that when you took half of the genetics from each parent you took a 50/50 chance on the desirable traits of each parent, and with your rotten luck, you got pups that had neither the super fuel injection of the Muktuks nor the super linkage of the Ugruks. In the roulette wheel of genetics, you have to get two balls to land on your number, not just one. (Huh?)

So, you start to see what line breeding is about. You try to breed dogs with similar ancestors to preserve whatever-the-heck it is that makes them so darn good. But as in everything in dogs, balance is the key. Don't go breeding littermates together or dogs back to their parents, or their parents' littermates. Nothing kinky allowed here. Beyond that it gets to be more art than science. It's said if it works it's line breeding and if it doesn't it's inbreeding, but we want to shy away from the stuff we're pretty sure is going to be called inbreeding at the end of the day.

Even as I write this, I'm checking my sidearm, glancing over my shoulder and out in the woods, for pure-breed fanciers in business suits who probably want me drawn and quartered for suggesting line breeding. Listen, if you are messing around with dogs from a gene pool so limited that every blessed one of them ends up exactly the same size, and white with little black spots, I can understand why you would never line breed them. You might get one with pink spots for cryin'-out-loud!

All kidding aside, the dogs we are breeding have enough genetic diversity to breed fairly close and have no problems, and the greatest benefit is a higher percentage of really good dogs.

Don't go hog wild breeding dogs, either. You will probably average about six pups a litter, more if you are fooling around with hounds and pointers, which I hope you aren't. So at six pups a pop, how many can you feed, care for, and train? Until you start winning races, you won't sell many either, especially the ones you don't want.

You have probably seen the ads:

> *For Sale: A few "special dogs," [rejects] from a developing kennel [which has yet to produce a competitive team]. All have sweet personalities, cute eyes, but a little "inconsistent" about pulling [lazy]. Make offer, won't last long. [I bet.]*

Well anyway, that's what the ad says to me, so don't think you are going to sell a lot of dogs until you prove your kennel in some serious races. Don't go overboard on your numbers of dogs.

There again, a little name-dropping will help immensely in selling or placing dogs that don't fit into your team. Better to offer a young dog for sale attached to the name of a top winning musher, than out of a dog from Harry Halfwit from Huffin, Alaska.

Dog Acquisition

Females in the heat pen. You need good pens to raise sled dogs.

As far as the process of breeding one dog to another, I assume you realize it takes a boy dog and a girl dog. It is possible to breed a female on her first heat, which can happen earlier than six months of age but usually between nine months and a year. Some males will produce by a year old for sure, but I rarely breed either that young anyway. I always want to breed proven dogs, and that doesn't happen by one year of age.

Females will come into heat pretty often the first couple of years. Some of them seem to spend nearly as much time in the heat pen as out, but it's probably about every three to four months. Later it will average twice a year, and some are every six months like clockwork. As they reach about seven years old, the time between heats usually gets longer, or they may skip a heat altogether. We recently had a successful litter from an eleven-year-old mother and a ten-year-old father, but that's getting up there in age for both of them.

Check the female for bloody vaginal discharge indicating the heat cycle has started. Chain her inside the heat pen immediately, whether or not you plan on breeding her. Lock the gate latch. If she isn't chained she could dig or climb out. If the latch isn't locked or pinned a loose male could knock it open with a little persistence. Take absolutely zero chances. The wrong male breeding your chosen brood bitch is as bad as the wrong girl turning up pregnant.

I'm tempted to get up on my soapbox again here, but all I need to say is use a little sense. Build some good doggone pens and control your doggone heaties! Breed the ones you want bred to the best males, and don't have accidents! There, that felt good.

When there are females in heat around, your peaceful property will take on a new personality. Females will howl for hours. Males will bark all night. Even the dogs will misbehave! They will run in circles and slam against their collars, wearing their feet to shreds. Heavy dog houses will tumble aside. Stout chains will succumb. Ordinary fencing fabric will be only a minor obstacle. Dogs will bite bloody their dearest kennel mates. And your cheery disposition will take a trip south, I'll wager.

There is nothing wrong with spaying and neutering some of these maniacs to help maintain calm and prevent unwanted litters. But then again, there is nothing wrong with leaving them intact for future breeding stock if you can control them. Don't get bullied by the "spay/neuter everything in sight" crowd. Altering your dogs won't hurt their performance as sled dogs one bit (and in some cases it significantly improves them), but it does put a serious damper on their participation in your breeding program, and could also make it harder to sell or place the dog with another kennel.

I suppose that paragraph could "disappoint" some of my more pet-oriented colleagues. Well, that's the truth of it where sled dogs are concerned. But as a pet owner I can't understand why you wouldn't spay or neuter your

Dog Acquisition

dog. They're a royal pain when someone's in heat, and who gets to deal with the unwanted pups?

Your female will have a little bit of bloody red discharge for roughly a week (could be two days, could be two weeks), then pronounced swelling takes place, indicating time for breeding. There may be a yellowish or brownish discharge at this stage. If you are planning on breeding this one, don't get out any herbs, incense, medical equipment, or bondage contraptions. You don't have to play music or dim the lights either. If the chosen male is interested and the female stands still, gets her tail out of the way, and otherwise cooperates, then they will breed. If any of the above doesn't happen, put the male away and wait for two days. Don't just leave the male in there. You want to actually see the breedings and record the dates, not guess or surmise that they must have bred.

Supervise the breeding. Once they have hooked up, be sure the male gets his leg over and they stand stern to stern. The female may indicate a little discomfort for a few seconds, but not much more. Take a short lead and snap the girl to the fence, and stand by until they unhitch, which could be up to 45 minutes (an hour and 15 minutes is the longest I have seen), but usually not that long. It is a good idea to turn the doghouse door against the fence or up on top, so neither one gets cold feet and tries to dive into the doghouse during breeding. If it happens after they hook up it can hurt one or both of them.

Once both parties consent, and you have a breeding, repeat the breeding every other day as long as both cooperate. If you get one breeding at the right time, well that's all it takes, but you can't be sure when the right time is, not with farmer methods anyhow. This way you will never miss. The way I understand it, the sperm can hang around and still do the trick for a couple of days, and once everything is all set with the female, the eggs can hold out for a couple of days as well. Breed them together every two days and even if you missed the last one by mere moments, the next one still scores. I guess it must be a little like horseshoes or hand grenades.

Don't hold the female and make her breed if she doesn't want to. I know with some breeds of dogs they do all sorts of strange stuff with tables and stands and thermometers and teasers, etc. Stuff I could never explain to my eleven-year-old son. Leave that to the fanciers and be satisfied to let nature take her course, where sled dogs are concerned. Trust me. If the girl doesn't want to breed, the time is not right, and holding her for the male won't result in pups anyway. I know for sure the female can experience trauma and tearing from this type of "mating" and you will hate yourself in the morning.

They are usually receptive to breeding for about a week to ten days; though I have had females stand for as little as one day and as much as two weeks. Once they are no longer interested it takes another one to two weeks for her vaginal swelling to reduce and for the males to no longer be interested. Keep her in the pen the full time. You don't want her accidentally bred to a second male because you took her out too soon.

Every once in a while, I have seen a male that doesn't seem interested in the female at first. She may be practically backing up under him, tail flagging, and he just ignores her. I know, I know, Brokeback Mountain, Elton John, whatever. I see it sometimes with older and more experienced studs, and you start to think, maybe the old boy needs Viagra or something. Just when you think you are going to miss the breeding, you put him in the pen with the female one last time before recruiting another stud, and bada-boom. The more experienced studs seem to know the right day and aren't impressed with the girl who struts her stuff a week early.

Now, that's all real simple until you get into the whole pack mentality thing. Remember, I'm supposed to be the

Dog Acquisition

Big Dog here. Well, when it comes to breeding in the pack, only the Big Dog is supposed to sire pups, so occasionally a male won't breed if the pack leader is around (meaning me). Some of your males could care less about that, and as long as they can jump the fence or break the chain, they by gumbo, are going to be fathers. Sometimes though, that part of the order is strongly ingrained in the male dog you are trying to breed. I don't know if you have, or ever will see this, but I have, so I guess I can talk about it.

I have a dog that any long distance driver intent on winning would be well advised to sell the house, truck and the china to buy this dog, except he isn't for sale. Well, depends on how nice a truck you've got. This dog would run through a blizzard to the moon for me. He's high strung all right, but he's happy, and he likes me. Anyway, I breed him a lot as you might have guessed and the pups are just what I'm looking for. But when it comes to breeding, he won't do it if he thinks I'm watching. If I go to the far side of the yard and pretend to be really busy with something else he may breed, but he may not. He has been in the pen with a girl in full heat and he barely sniffs her. He just lies down and rivets his eyes on me and watches. If I hang around, he will lay there looking at me all afternoon. Once I got concerned we were going to miss the cycle on a particular female I really wanted to breed, so I got to paying close attention. What in blazes is wrong with you, boy? Then I caught on. I started walking back to the shop, about 100 yards away, and he just kept staring at me. I got to the door and stood there for a while, and he's still lying down, just watching me. I go inside and shut the door to watch from the window and you know what happened. I no sooner got the door shut and we had a tie.

I offer my (tongue in cheek) apologies here to reproduction experts everywhere. I hope they don't know where I live. There are well-done and thoughtful volumes out there on dog breeding, and I encourage you to read them when you have time. But if your females are already coming into heat, just do it my way for now. These animals have been reproducing for a very long time without our help, thank you very much, and I'm sure they will breed in your kennel too. (I think there is a Pug breeder sneaking through the bushes outside!)

Recycled Dogs

I'm really not interested in stepping on anyone's toes here, and given that this writing is not likely to even make the Mukluk Telegraph Best Seller List, let alone a dime in profit, I sure have no motivation to do so. I just want people starting out and hungry for knowledge to get a fair shake. The only ones who really know what's up are often reluctant to share the information and sometimes the sport as a whole suffers.

Look, your job is to put together a great dog team. If you're running the Iditarod, it has to be a pretty remarkable group of athletes just to keep up with the field. You probably have limited resources available or earmarked for your dog expenses, and given that it costs exactly the same to care for a poor dog as for a good one, why on God's earth would you fill up your limited number of doghouses with dogs that someone else already decided weren't worth feeding? Maybe if you are a great trainer you can make something out of a few of them, I'm not saying you can't, but I still ask, why? There are two chances of these dogs being champions: slim and none. If your method of dog acquisition is to go down to the pound and load up everything that looks a little like a husky, as some have done, and you plan to keep each and every one of them until they die of old age, I'd say you are a wonderful person with a big heart, but without a prayer of developing a decent dog team.

Dog Acquisition

Yes, there are stories of the pound dog "done good" (according to the story teller), but that sure doesn't make the animal shelter an ideal place to shop if you are planning to be good at this someday.

The first time somebody said to me "I run rescues," was years ago at the Fairbanks mushing symposium. It seemed an odd thing to interject in the middle of a conversation about sled dogs so I'm sure I looked puzzled.

"Right on," I replied. "My brother does rescue work too; he's a fireman and an E.M.T."

Obviously there are many different scenarios under which a guy could come by a good dog for free. In fact, if one or two kennels I can think of got in a bind for dog food and started giving away their best dogs, I may just send one of the boys over to have a look. (After writing this section, you wouldn't expect me to actually show up myself, would you?) But mostly, free dogs from almost any source will just saddle you with responsibility and won't do much to get you down the trail.

Remember, you are not collecting pets here. You are assembling a team of top athletes.

Pet Parents, Beware

For thousands of years, the weaker dogs in this lifestream were eliminated from the gene pool. No surprise, it happens in every species on earth. Well, not humans or our pets, but every other species has performance requirements for survival. That's what keeps the species strong. Somewhere along the way, people have blurred the lines between humans and our pets. Now it seems not only humans but also house cats and pet dogs are guaranteed long life no matter what. Folks get all mixed up and pretty soon they look at animals from a human perspective rather than an animal perspective. A few generations back these dogs would've had two choices: Run with the pack, or starve. It's a principle that has served your dog's wild cousins for millennia, and they never knew they needed to be rescued.

I think a lot of this confusion is brought about intentionally by some who stand to make a lot of money by making you feel guilty about animals. Not only the whackos trying to whip up a frenzy over one thing or another and then quickly pass the hat. No, there are some animal care professionals and veterinarians that want you to think you are a "pet parent" not an animal owner. Of course, if you are a pet parent, then the animal is your "child", thus no expense must be spared for the medical care of your child. Here's where we go to the lunatic fringe– animal care professionals encouraging animal owners to spend big bucks on kidney transplants or cataract surgery for a twelve-year-old dog? To me that's just wrong. In fact, any expense that exceeds the dollar value of the dog is suspect in my book.

Certainly not all vets are guilty of this pet parent deception, but plenty are. I kind of like veterinarians who are farm girls or old rodeo cowboys.

Now I'm not so dense that I don't realize the emotional value people put on their pets, and I am not fit to judge another animal owner's decisions or actions. (I do wish some others afforded that same respect to dog mushers, however.) In fact, with very few exceptions, the value of any animal is exactly the value placed on it by that animal's owner. No more. No less

I just don't like other folks manipulating our love of animals for unreasonable profit. A very wise lady came up with the best idea ever, regarding unreasonably large expenditures on animals, and overcoming the guilt and loss some people feel when they have to put down their pet. We were talking one time about how you can get almost any medical procedure for an animal that you can for a human, and the figure $16,000 was mentioned as the price of a kidney transplant for a dog. She suggested the dog owner should have the dog euthanized, and donate $16,000 to Children's Hospital, and then spend $79 to adopt a new pet from the pound. Amen Mom, Amen.

This same "pet-as-your-child" mentality also gets promoted by those who don't have as much to gain from it. They just think that others expect them to think that way. They don't want to seem like a primitive brute, so they tell my dog to "go to Daddy," presumably meaning me. My revulsion turns to fear as I wonder what my wife must think of my other family!

Other folks have a holier-than-thou attitude and perceive themselves as more highly evolved than primitive brutes like me because they "get it" that they are pet parents and I don't. Well, so be it among the fanciers of the world. As for me, there is no confusion between who is a family member and who is an animal. My obligations and responsibilities to those two separate groups are very, very different.

There is a vast difference between animals and humans and what is a good life for one is not the same as for the other. I have heard it asked, "How would you like to have to run 1000 miles?" to which I would reply, "Not at all. I'm glad I'm not a dog. Say, I wonder how the dog would like to prepare my federal tax return for me."

In sled dog circles we have gotten ourselves afraid of a paper tiger in the form of animal rights activists because their numbers soar to the double digits and they have a lot of internet aliases. Be assured that the common citizen does not hold extreme views, and the few who do, have been lied to (they read it on the internet). They usually change their minds once they conduct extensive research, like actually see a dog team. I believe most people are at least a little queasy deep down about the whole pet-as-your-child concept anyway. If you apply a little imagination to the idea you quickly envision a world run by animals, with no responsibilities or requirements, lording it over a bunch of pathetic guilt-ridden pet parents!

Some in sled dog circles are so eager to prove to the world that they are not primitive brutes that they begin spouting the same nonsense, until even those who know better are almost forced to lie and act like pet parents, at least when the cameras are rolling!

Okay, okay, I'll calm down, but I don't want you adopting a bunch of "inconsistent pullers with sweet personalities and cute eyes," okay? Promise? You will probably never know the absolute elation of running a great dog team if you start out that way. Start out with the best young stuff you can. If you possess a need to nurture, years from now, if you're lucky, there will be an unwavering, lion-hearted champion who has spent his whole life hauling your sorry behind through everything in the arctic and beyond. As the sun goes down on his racing years, offer this magnificent animal your affection and gratitude and nurture him as long as he can reasonably enjoy life and eat your expensive dog food. He has earned it.

Three:
Puppies

Whelping

If you want a complete list of everything you could get all worked up over on the subject of whelping check out some of the books out there, and you may change your mind on the whole idea. Some of them make you feel as if you need a hospital emergency room available to have puppies. In my experience, however, the whole process is so easy that you should have nothing to worry about.

The pups will come about 63 days after conception, but not necessarily 63 days after breeding, because the actual fertilization could have been a couple of days later. About four weeks out you should double the mother's food as long as she will eat it. In our kennel this will amount to about 2½ cups of Blackwood 2000 commercial dog food plus about two pounds of salmon per day. Have good weight on her when the pups are born. Some moms can get pretty skinny after nursing the litter for six or seven weeks.

Anyway, the ol' gal will probably start looking pretty big about two weeks before the pups are due. Put her in a pen with a whelping box with bedding, preferably wood shavings, but straw will do. The bedding is mostly to absorb moisture and should be changed right after the birthing is done and regularly thereafter. Never let her have pups while on a chain. She may be restricted by the chain and not be able to reach her mouth where she needs to for delivery. This could endanger both pups and Mom. Realize that as soon as a pup enters the world between the mothers back legs, the mom must use her teeth to separate the pup from the placenta or birth sack and sever the umbilical cord with her teeth. She also uses her tongue to clean off the pup and stimulate the pup's circulation. A chain can definitely interfere with all of this. Also, mothers on chains tend to drag the pups out on the ground with the chain and some are not too prompt about getting them back in the house.

The whelping box is basically a big doghouse (30" by 36", 24" high), and should have two-by-fours screwed on edge all the way around the inside, about four inches up from the bottom like a little shelf. This keeps the mom from crushing or suffocating a pup that may accidentally get behind her in the corner of the box. It's handy to have the roof on hinges to get at the pups easily for handling.

The female may start acting agitated, perhaps chewing and digging holes, a couple of days before delivery. Try to keep the holes filled in so she actually uses your cute little whelping box setup, but lots of dogs have been born in a hole in the ground with no noted long-term ill effects. After they are born you can probably move them into the house, no problem. She almost certainly won't eat for about 24 hours before birthing begins so you should know when she is close to delivering.

You can probably impress your wife. "You know Honey, I've been out in the yard meditating and I just have a feeling those pups are coming in the next 24 hours." Sure enough, you are big man in the kennel tomorrow night.

Puppies

I once got a frantic call from a neighbor who was a new musher, when one of his gals was whelping. He was sure that she was a deranged killer since she had buried her pups alive. Upon questioning, it turns out she had dug a nice basement apartment under her house, birthed the pups just fine, and when she stepped out to powder her nose, had a slight unexpected cave in. This caused the house to settle into the hole a little and she couldn't quite get back into the new nursery. With the help of "He with the Opposable Thumbs," the family was reunited and all was well.

I've heard of plenty of mushers staying up all night and worrying over the birthing process. Frankly, in dozens of litters, I've never had one that needed any help.

I don't want them on a chain for the birthing process, but I don't favor leaving them unconfined either. There was the time we had one loose in the yard and she was sticking close so we figured she would have the pups in her house. On the big day she was nowhere to be found. Eventually we heard something under the cabin and sure enough, that's where she and the pups were. Problem was, the space was so small there was no way for me to get to them. Luckily I had small kids at the time that could squeeze in there and drag the little beggars out. It could have been bad too, if she'd run off somewhere to have the pups.

I guess the only time it takes a little more fuss is in the winter. In the summer if the whelping box is dry, the temperature should be plenty warm. If you're around, it's nice if you can grab an old towel and dry the pups off right away, but I wouldn't miss poker night over it if it's warm out. Winter is different. Put the mom in the shop, garage, porch, or better yet, the handler cabin for the birth until the pups get a couple of days old.

Whelping box with hinged lid.

Pups in whelping box with safety rails.

Raising Pups

I am peeking out the curtains and the hair is raising on the back of my neck again, as everyone who is a medical person, dog fancier or mother of any kind is after my hide over that last section. "How could you be so casual or cavalier about the birth of your pups? Shouldn't you take precautions? Have a veterinarian standing by?"

This birthing process is one of the fascinating things about these dogs. A brand new, first-time mother knows exactly what to do. It's one of those instinctive miracles. They know what to do, and they can't help but do it. They have no choice. Thousands of years of life-stream demands that they do certain things and they don't even have to think about it. I guess I have heard of mothers that don't accept the pups, but I have never seen it, and it's very rare among sled dogs. I suspect it may have something to do with a nutritional problem, and the mother senses she can't care for the pups.

Occasionally you have a runt or weaker pup that doesn't make it past a couple of days. Don't let it get you down too badly. Look at this from the animal perspective. Here you have six or so pups in a pile, all headed toward the dairy bar. Noses outstretched, 24 feet digging and clawing. They have to keep "running" with the pack to get to the goods. If one is too weak to belly up to the bar, the other 20 digging, clawing legs push him back. It's amazing. In nature, these animals face (and depend upon) the law of the survival of the fittest nearly from the moment of birth.

Once, as I stood watching these little guys all running in place almost as a unit, heading toward their next meal, I was struck by the fact that this is what these dogs have been doing as predators for centuries. Run as a pack until you get your next meal. And that's what they will do as racing dogs. Run together to the next checkpoint. Running in a team just suits these guys to a tee. What else on earth would they do?

Peach's pups "running" for their next meal.

Puppies

One of the first things you have to do is get the dew-claws off of the pups. The dewclaws are the floppy little toes on the inside of the upper foot that look like they are auditioning to be thumbs. They are always present on the front feet and sometimes, though rarely, on the backs. These have to come off because they are right where the strap of a dog bootie will hit later. If you have never done it, get someone to show you. You could use a vet, but if you do, be sure you learn how to do it yourself for next time.

I use a large toenail clipper and just cut 'em off. Then you will see a little soft bone in there. It's really just a little nub. You have to get that out of there, or else it will grow back in one form or another. Have some styp-tic powder, trace mineral drops, or other blood-stop stuff handy. Sometimes they don't bleed, sometimes they do. Make sure they all stop bleeding before you leave them. I've heard vets say to dewclaw them at two or three days. I think they are convinced it would hurt less at an early age or something, but I tell you, they can bleed a lot and holler quite a bit at that age. It's better to do them at six days. They don't cry much, or bleed much. The little bone is easier to get out, and it's less traumatic for the mother. Thank you "Dr. Mitch."

Once summer while I was zigging and zagging all over the state, a litter was missed until it was ten days old. I went ahead as usual and it worked out just the same as the six day olds, at least with that litter. I suspect that's about the time that little bone starts attaching and forming a real toe out of the dewclaw, so ten days could be too late for some litters.

For the first four weeks you should take a close look at the mother at least early every morning, last thing at night, and once in between. It's rare, but they can get a low calcium condition called hypocalcaemia that is fatal to the mother. It's not a dietary deficiency, but as a lot of calcium is going to milk production, something goes hay-wire in the mom's system and she doesn't make the necessary adjustments to preserve enough calcium for her own body. Since calcium is necessary for just about everything, the mom can get into big trouble in just a few hours after the first symptoms are visible. The one I had got lethargic, uncoordinated, and eventually paralyzed. The 4:00 am vet visit was a little too late and it didn't end well. It was doubly sad when I learned that a quick blood analysis and a calcium injection would have saved her, if we had been a little earlier. The pups then would have to be bottle fed or adopted by another mother, if you have one nursing.

Keep feeding the mother double or even more, and don't let her ever run out of water. They go through a lot of water, and the nursing mother that gets really thin-looking may need water more than anything. By three weeks provide water for the pups too, in a low dish. A small hubcap will do. (Do cars even have hubcaps anymore?) Start feeding them soft food by four weeks. The back of the bag may tell you to feed only a couple of kibbles per pup at first, but they are probably already stuffing themselves on Mom's food by now and I have never seen a problem with it. I guess that presumes you are feeding a high quality food.

About six to seven weeks old they will be ready to wean. If the mother hasn't weaned them already, just tie the mom back in her old place in the yard. She may have some separation anxiety for a day or two, but it won't last long. You can put her back in at night for a few nights especially if she is keeping you awake with her carrying on. This works well if you are trying to get the pups weaned before the mom got around to doing it herself.

From there on feeding the pups is a bit of an art. You should feed a high quality kibble like Blackwood 2000,

Puppies

plus a little fish or meat for variety. Feed the pups twice a day for about two weeks after weaning or until about nine weeks of age. Then, being the mean so-and-so that I am, I go to feeding only once a day for pups. Ignore the bag. Ignore the vet. Just feed them as much as they will "wolf down" (interesting term there) in about thirty seconds, once a day. You want these guys to eat everything you give them immediately. Food should last about thirty seconds in the bowl. Gradually increase the amount, as they get bigger, but don't let them get fat or slow down on the eating pace. You are training piranhas here. This is very important so they always, always, eat what you give them right away. On races you want the dogs to eat as soon as possible when you feed, not mess around about it. Good eaters are made, mostly, in the puppy pen.

Every time you feed your pups give them a distinct verbal signal. We use an upbeat "pup, pup, pup" call as the food hits the feed pan. It comes in handy anytime you want to call your dogs back to you. I once had a loose dog running around McGrath during my 24-hour layover on the Iditarod, and this is how I finally caught the bugger. I felt a little odd, I'll admit, following a 55-pound dog around town calling "Pup, pup, pup!"

You have a few meds to give when they are little too. I use Anthelban to worm them at two, four, seven, ten, and fourteen weeks, and roughly every month thereafter. I vaccinate at six, nine, twelve and sixteen weeks, using parvo vaccine the first two times and five-way vaccine the last two. You can buy this stuff in bulk from pet supply catalogues. Check this out with the manufacturer and a vet so you know what you are doing. Rabies vaccinations must be done by a professional in most places, but you can save some money by taking advantage of free state-sponsored rabies vaccination clinics. Check with animal shelters about this.

You need good pens to raise dogs. Put females in heat in a dog-proof pen and chain them in there. You would be amazed at the escape stunts both males and females can pull off if someone is in heat. I use chain link fence because dogs can tear right through the welded mesh stuff. I have several puppy pens, 20 feet square, eight feet high, and I pretty much keep each litter separate. There is a three-foot space between each pen and the next one. I used to have pens separated just by wire, but then I had pups sticking their legs through and getting grabbed by the bigger pups in the next pen. It wasn't pretty. I also have some stuff in there for pups to play on, like tires and pallets and maybe a log. It all helps later.

When dogs are chained inside pens, make sure there is no way they can get over the fence and hang themselves on the chain. Eight-foot high fences should take care of it, but still, make sure they can't climb on the house and try to jump over.

Four:
Early Education

Spend time playing with your pups. Take them out for walks. It's also good to teach them something, even if it's just to come or follow you or a signal to get back in the pen. That way they learn early on that their relationship with people involves them responding and obeying.

One of the best things we did for our pups was to build a big exercise pen or run pen. It's a couple of hundred feet across, and we put a few pups in there at a time to run around. We put an older dog in there with them and it seems to bring order to the whole bunch. The older dog runs around and the pups chase him instead of chewing on each other. It's not good to raise pups in a small pen only, even if it's 20 feet across The run pen is the best idea I've found to exercise a lot of pups without putting them at risk.

You can free run them some, but after a certain age they just run too far away, and it's not worth risking their safety. We live a mile from the highway, and we've had pups caught and corralled in a horse trailer at the store four miles down the road. We've had them gone overnight, too. I'm not a real fan of free running my dogs; partly because I can't keep up with them once they get bigger. Remember, I'm supposed to be the Big Dog in the pack. We did it with a four-wheeler for a while, but one ran in front of the machine, and got hit, so we quit that too. Everybody I know who has their sled dogs loose a lot has stories (not often repeated) about losing one or more dogs at some time or another. Pointers and hounds are probably a little better about sticking around than huskies, so some kennels probably do all right with it. I know some people also have the ideal setup with water to swim in and no roads around, and it works for them, but for most situations I think the run pen is the best idea for young dogs before you start hooking them up.

If you have several litters or there is any chance of mixing up the pups, you should put litter-identifying collars on them at an early age, even in the pens. We often have several litters around of similar age at some point in the summer, and have had mix-ups before.

A big brown male pup once spent most of an afternoon using his littermates as chew toys, so one of my boys tried to do the right thing. He attempted to move the pup into the next pen with another litter of slightly older pups. He got him in there all right, but the pup proceeded to kick butt on the bigger pups as well. The kid decided to put the pup back in the other pen. Reports vary on what happened next, but apparently one gate didn't latch and the other was being opened to deposit the pup, resulting in a double-barreled scattergun of charging half-grown dogs. All the pups from both pens were loose. The pups loved the idea of running around making all the big dogs bark, and the boy spent about an hour capturing them all. Upon reincarceration they were just pitched into whichever pen was closest. Never deterred from his original mission, the boy decided to tie up the offending brown male puppy to solve his problem once and for all. Once I got home, he reluctantly reported the situation to me. I went to the yard and found twelve well-exercised pups resting peacefully and one forlorn little female pup on a chain. I think we eventually got them back with their litters, but we had the darnedest time with the boy/girl count until we checked the one he had tied up.

Even if you have only one litter in each pen, put a light chain around every pup's neck, and fasten it with a small color coordinated zip-tie. If you try regular collars at this stage the pups will eat each other's collars off and mess you up. When you tie them up use color coordinated collars or mark the collars for each litter. Don't leave one litter unmarked, because then if another collar comes off you could be in the same boat as my young son.

Tie the pups up around six months of age. If there starts to be a lot of growling and fighting in the pen you may have to separate some, but they can make an awful ruckus and still not really hurt each other. If nobody is getting hurt or crowded out of the feed dish there is no harm in a little rumble in the pen now and then. Be sure though, that everyone is digging in at feeding time. You could have one that gets intimidated and doesn't eat enough.

Continue to use the run pen once you tie up the pups. They will probably get less exercise on the chain, so try to get them in the big pen daily if you can.

Feeding Young Dogs

Continue feeding once a day and adjust each one's feed to its needs. As a result of the group-feeding thing in the pen you may have some fatter than others, so make adjustments. We switch over from Blackwood 2000 to Blackwood 7000 about the time we tie up the pups and feed about 2½ cups per dog per day. If we have plenty of fish available we often feed Blackwood and salmon on alternate days, especially in the summer when it's warmer and the work load is less. Be sure every dog eats all of its food right away. Remember, you are training the dog to eat everything immediately so he will do the same thing on a race. Pups at this point are usually good eaters, unless you have already spoiled them in the pen.

Keep them a little thin. If you think dogs should look like most Americans these days, then you will train your dogs to be poor eaters. You should be able to make out the back couple of ribs under the hair, and even the hip bones will be protruding a little on most huskies. You don't want to see the vertebrae prominently, or see too many of the ribs, but I guarantee you if you raise high-strung racing dogs you will have some that meet that description as adolescents and they will still be perfectly healthy. Some of them just don't put on weight at this age no matter what you do.

Again, if the dog doesn't eat everything in about 30 seconds, do not just leave food laying around thinking he may eat more at a later time. Take the food away. Give the dog only clear water the next day and half rations the following day. Resume regular feeding the fourth day. Do this no matter how thin you think the dog is. Okay, if he's sick or whatever that's obviously a different story, but once you've fed dogs for a while you will know what I mean. This regimen or some variation thereof, is what I call F.A.T.; that's Food Appreciation Training.

Sometimes the thin dogs are the worst eaters. Profound, eh? You think, "Well doggone it, he has to eat!" (Same rationale justifies a second piece of cake for us, right?) So you leave food there or get other treats to entice the dog. All you are doing is encouraging this dog's pain-in-the-backside behavior, while he trains you to his wishes, rather than the reverse. Look, nothing encourages eating like hunger. You have to change his mind about food or he will probably be a skinny, poor eater all his life.

You can feed twice a day for particularly thin dogs as a way to get more food into them and keep good digestion. I don't ever advocate feeding them more often than that unless it's on a race. The dog starts to think he's trained you! If he doesn't feel like eating now it's no big deal because his "servant" will be back again before you know it with another chance to eat. I think that works against good eating habits. The dog needs to view feeding as a big deal, an opportunity not to be missed. Remember, for thousands of years their ancestors have survived by running, sometimes for days, catching prey and eating all they could hold at one time. Our dogs are pampered, even on a once a day feeding schedule!

Don't try to get by with cheap dog food. Look, if you figure out the calories and the digestibility of the high-end dog foods, you will find they are the better deal anyway. Your dog will be healthier and perform better with better food, no question. You will have less to clean up in the yard too, which in itself is a good reason to buy a better food.

Feed the amount recommended on the bag, plus at least a half-pound of raw meat per dog per day, during training. I prefer to feed a red meat like beef or horse during training since most commercial dog foods are based on poultry and fish proteins. Add a high quality fat supplement as well, in cold weather and under hard working conditions, such as up to a quarter-pound of beef fat and a tablespoon of corn oil per dog. Add the fat gradually to maintain stool consistency until the dogs get used to it.

Lately some food manufacturers are promoting their food as being so good you don't have to feed meat with it. Well, I suppose you don't have to, but you had better if you want to get the best out of your team. There are some things a working dog needs in his diet that can't be provided in any cooked, processed meal. Feed meat.

We'll go into detail on feeding working dogs a little later.

Harness Breaking

Well, the big moment has come. You're going to hook the little beggars up and go for a run. You've seen the beautiful photography of Iditarod and other racing teams. Sixteen evenly paired dogs flowing in unison as the sled and driver skim over the trail without a sound. Well, forget about it. This will look more like a jailbreak at the zoo on wheelchair appreciation day. First thing I'm going to tell you is to get some help. If you don't have a handler, sober up the neighbor, and haul him over. Get somebody.

I like to hook them up for the first time at about nine to twelve months of age. Actually, in the spring after racing, we just hook up the oldest of last summer's pups. The youngest ones may have to wait and get hooked up later on the four-wheeler.

I hook up two good leaders who will hold the line out straight, and up to six pups behind them, to the sled, four-wheeler or snow machine. If you don't have those leaders, well, you're going to need them, but for now you can tie them off to something so the pups don't pull them around backwards and implode your team. Hook the pups up as fast as you can, with as much help as you've got. Have the neighbor or somebody keep them from strangling themselves or eating each other while you and your handler, your spouse, girlfriend, kid, and whomever else you can recruit get them on the towline. I prefer to hook pups next to pups for the first run. Some drivers like to put a pup next to an older dog, and there's a time for that, but not right at first because they may be intimidated by an older dog and you could ruin the pup right there. Don't worry if they jump the line or get tangled up and leave yourself a few extra spots in the towline so you can run at least a couple of them single-file if the puppy fights get out of hand. You can teach them to behave later. The whole idea here is to get them hooked up and let them do what they were born to do. Run. Nobody has to show them that.

Oh yeah. They will chew the heck out of your gear. You need a towline that's made right, with both tug lines and necklines. If it's right, it's very hard for them to turn all the way around as long as the leaders hold the main line tight. This is important right at first, until they figure out which way they are supposed to go. I use the extra heavy cable main line sections and light chain as necklines for puppy training. They can't chew loose, and they aren't wrecking my racing lines.

Well, that's about it. Oh yeah, go ahead and take off, take a handler with you, and don't forget to untie the leaders.

I did say take off. What I mean is creep forward. Top speed, three miles per hour. After going 100 feet, stop. Yes, 100 feet. Encouragement and pets all around, pull their legs out of each other's harness and go again. This time go 200 feet. Stop, give pets, untangle as best you can. Next go 400 feet, a little faster, and stop again. Now they are getting the hang of it. Give profuse pets and encouragement all around. If they are all going forward, you are ready for a quarter-mile, a little faster. Then a half-mile. For us that will be about the turn-around loop for the first run and we can nearly always run back home without much stopping, at say, six miles an hour.

Second run will look about the same. Basically a mess going forward, but you won't have to stop much, just keep it slow. By the third run you will see them start to understand a little about the lines, harness, avoiding tangles, and generally what the heck is going on.

Here's the key. Do not frighten or intimidate them out of running. I don't think we can really teach them to run, but I know we can ruin them if we mess up the first few runs. Let them have fun, and don't worry about tangles or bad behavior. Don't yell or act freaked out. Always be calm and just laugh at the little morons, no matter what. You have to tell them right here that mushing is fun and they are the lucky dogs that get to do it. Watch especially for a pup who is being intimidated by a more dominant pup next to him. Stop and rearrange the team right away. Don't let him get so scared he won't run. You could ruin him right there if he falls or gets knocked down. Now he thinks mushing is bad, all because of a bully next to him.

We harness break dozens of pups every season, and it has been years since we had one that wouldn't run right away. I can remember one notable slow-starter, however.

I had purchased a youngster from Joe Redington Sr., and right away named him Joe Joe. He was supposed to be two years old, but since he kept on growing after we got him, I'm sure he was only a yearling. He had never been hooked up. Where I was harness breaking my pups we usually went over a bridge, and he did fine until we got to that bridge, where he pretty much laid down and quit. I figured it was the bridge, so I planned to go a different way the next time, but Joe Joe was so afraid we were going to the bridge again he laid down just out of the yard. I couldn't run him so I sent one of the kids back home with him on a leash. I had seen all I needed to see of that worthless dog.

Luckily for all of us, Joe Joe was a cute Siberian-looking dog and smaller than the others. Pretty well behaved too. The kids were young, but they wanted to have their own dog to mush, all by themselves. They asked about Joe Joe, and almost without hearing them I said,

Early Education

"Uh-huh." What did I care what the kids did with that worthless dragger? What could they do to him anyway, ruin him? Hah! Besides, he's going back to Joe, next time I get up that way.

It was about a week later, I drove in the driveway and nearly collided with a dog team, or at least what a seven-year-old might call a dog team. As I hit the brakes, I was involved in a flawless head-on pass with a cute Siberian looking dog pulling two kids on a big old cardboard refrigerator box, with a milk crate somehow tied on top, or at least on the side that was usually the top. I watched in disbelief as they marched on out the driveway without a pause. Not only was Joe Joe in lead (he was the only dog) but he was pulling hard enough to drag that huge box and two hollering kids, climbing on and falling off, doing their best to weight it down.

Joe Joe just needed to go on a few runs where he didn't get scared by the bridge. The kids and their "training methods" were just right– short runs, going slow, stopping a lot, and having fun. Joe Joe became one of the best dogs I ever had. He finished six Iditarods in lead, including fourth place in 1998. At this writing he is fifteen years old, deaf and nearly blind, but still putting on miles tottering non-stop around the perimeter of his pen. He's still a traveler. He still barks when we hook up teams, too. It sort of makes a guy a little emotional. Well, not me actually, but I could see how it might make someone else a little emotional. But he had his day, and it was all because of a couple of kids and a refrigerator box.

Joe Joe (on right) in lead with Dolphin. Two of our past greats.

Forward Orientation

There is one very important concept here, in everything you do with your dogs on a run. I call it "forward orientation." There are really two parts to this concept. First there is the forward oriented attitude and natural inclination of a good sled dog to travel forward down the trail. Second is the idea of the musher training the team with a forward oriented mindset to encourage the natural drive of the dogs.

Once they have been hooked up a few times they know what's going on. They know you are going to put on the harness, hook them to the line, and take off, in a direction away from the sled, four-wheeler, or whatever they are hooked to. All your training should be oriented forward. Don't tolerate a dog trying to turn around and visit the guy behind him, or go way off to the side either. Keep them straight forward, leaning into the harness.

The idea of forward orientation guides almost everything. When you hook up a pup the first few times, you should hook up the neckline first, pull back on the harness, and hook up the tug line. This will keep the pup from backing out of his harness, turning around, and making a trying situation worse, and right off the bat it keeps him pointed forward. After a few runs, however, he should know he is supposed to run and pull forward so I like to hook the tug up first, let the dog pull it tight going forward and then hook up the neckline. It may seem like a small thing but you have the dog going forward on his own during the process rather than having to forcibly pull him back to get the tug line hooked up. Even when I unhook the dogs, I like them to stand in place, snout forward, until I get the harness off. There isn't much difference in the dogs mind between spinning around and hauling me to his house while he has a harness on, and spinning around out on the trail and heading for his house. In my team the signal is the harness. If you're wearing one you'd best be aiming forward.

Out on the trail, forward orientation becomes even more important. You may see a dog that is running along okay, but his head is high and he is looking around or back at you or another dog. You need to fix this right away. Every step that dog takes doing anything that doesn't look forward oriented, he is learning that it's all right to mess around and not pull. It may be an easy fix, so move him around in the team until he is working right. Possible causes could include: Someone behind him or close in front of him has bit or growled at him in the past. There may be a female coming into heat, or just a female who isn't even in heat. There could be a small or passive male behind him, over whom our under-performer wants to assert dominance. The possibilities are many. Remember you have to think like a dog. What is going on in that dog's alleged mind to make him do whatever it is he's doing, rather than what I want him to do?

There are only a few factors that come into play in the dogs mind. It's not too complicated. Most folks will probably be offended when I tell you that pleasing you is not very high on his priority list. It's probably not even on the list unless you happen to want the same thing he wants. Luckily for us, the dogs we work with usually do want the same thing as we do – to run down the trail. You may have also made him want something through training, like a treat or affection, and he has learned to do some action on your command still remembering the treat, but it's not out of deep devotion to you.

It seems to me that big motivators for dogs are food, breeding, pack order, fear, physical comfort/affection, and habit, roughly in that order. My wife asserts that these motivators are the same for humans, especially a certain

Early Education

male human she knows. These motivators result in certain actions, some of them instinctive, such as running for great distances. Keep these motivators in mind as you "think like a dog," and use them to help understand what you are seeing in your team.

If you have the kind of dogs you should have, you will quickly see what forward orientation is all about, as soon as you run your pups. They will show you. As soon as you start moving the team forward for the very first time, with no prior harness training at all, the swarming mass will all of a sudden focus forward, and for some reason I can't really explain, they all begin to charge forward in a frenzy, as if their lives depended on it. Hmm, there may be something to that.

I have heard many mushers discuss a variety of problems with their dogs, which in my opinion, all relate to forward orientation. How do I stop my dog from looking back? Eating too much snow? Peeing on bushes? Playing around with his partner? Slacking off in the pulling department? Many will decide to try distractions, signals, shock collars, and the like to discourage an unwanted behavior.

Their fellow mushers will chime in with manure trucks full of anecdotal advice which they are sure is quite clever, if not helpful, but rarely will you hear someone discuss forward orientation. If the dog was as forward oriented as he should be, most of these problems would be minimized. The real problem isn't that he eats too much snow, looks back, pees on the bushes, etc., the real problem is that he isn't forward oriented enough. Later, when we get into training techniques, I'll give you a little "anecdotal advice" which may help, but most of the necessary ingredients come in the original package, and it's not easy to put it in later.

Forward oriented dogs don't get derailed by obstacles such as snowdrifts, open water, or other dog teams.

Forward oriented dogs don't hesitate to charge into checkpoints in races and they don't hesitate to charge out again. Forward oriented dogs pass and meet teams on the trail without fuss. They know that the goal is always ahead of them, so they keep charging forward. Forward orientation becomes a mindset and a state of being, and with that force in the blood stream of your team, many hurdles that send other mushers home with tail tucked won't even arise as an issue for you and your hearty trail mates.

About Face?

Another thing on forward orientation: Unless you are avoiding certain death, the Mongol horde, increased taxes or doing the dishes, don't ever turn your team around in place on the trail, ever. You can't imagine the grief you are creating by showing a young dog team that it's okay to turn around in place and head back toward home. Sometime later you will be stopped, getting out a chew of tobacco or taking a leak and look up to see your team in a tight horse-shoe configuration, your leaders hauling haunches for home. If that ever happens, you meet those leaders head on and make them think they just met certain death and the Mongol Horde, plus Godzilla. Oh, better zip up somewhere in there. And then swear off chewing as a punishment to yourself for having taught those dogs that doubling back is okay. Go to the trouble of making sure you have at least a good needles-eye loop to turn around on, but the bigger the better. In a perfect world you would have a trail set up kind of circular where you go out one way and come in another. I'm thinking this isn't a perfect world, so at least make sure you don't ever double them back around if there is any other way.

I know that some of you who already have dogs will be disappointed by this concept. You think you have really trained your dogs well, and one of your crowning achievements is your super-duper turn-around-in-place command. Seriously, you do not want your dogs to think that turning around in place is an option.

Somebody right now is saying "I've done turn-abouts for fifteen years and I've never had a problem. You just have to be smart like me and do it right, blah, blah, blah."

I guess if you never really put your dogs under stress you can get away with doing a lot of things wrong, but if you plan on training a long distance team capable of finishing the Iditarod and being competitive someday, and you turn them around in place, you are screwing up. Period.

Look, if you do lots of tough, long runs and really work them hard, you will eventually come across the situation where your loyal pack mates would rather call it quits and go home. I'm not saying they will, and I'm certainly not saying you should let them; just saying they will want to. So if you have them in the habit of turning around in place, even if they are supposed to wait for your special command, you will see them "mistake" something for that command sooner or later at the wrong time. In fact I have seen a so-called leader mistake a clear and distinct "haw" command for a "come gee" and he didn't even know the "come gee" command! I'd bet some of you that do turn around in the trail regularly, especially if you do it at the same spots often, don't even need a command to do it. I'd also bet that the turn happens a little sooner each time, and once you have twelve dogs turned around towards home, you sure don't bother to turn them back around to the original direction and reinforce your command!

If you turn around regularly in the same spot the dogs will anticipate it, making it very difficult to go past that spot later. If you change it up all the time, the dogs think any time you stop may be the turnaround, and that's not good either. And here's the worst of it: Turning around in place will cause the dogs to turn in a tepid performance for much of the run as they anticipate the turnaround. If your dogs are used to turning around in place, I believe your traveling speed will fall way off at some point during the run, even on new trails, as they anticipate, rather, attempt to cause, the turn around. You can't race with a team that thinks they are going to spin around and go back at any moment.

So if you think your leader is so well trained because he will turn around in place on command, here's a little challenge: Train your White Fang to take commands off the trail and make your own loop out in the snow, field, woods, or whatever for a turn around. If you are the guy who has been doing this for fifteen years, why haven't you bothered to make some kind of turnaround here and there in all that time? It doesn't take much. Just enough so it is completed while still going forward (away from the sled). You can even use somebody's driveway, and cut across the ditch if you have to.

The idea of turning around in place undermines the concept of forward orientation, which you have to adhere to with near religious fervor. It's like the rule of law in society; without it everything else breaks down.

Now I'll admit there are situations when even I might be open to the suggestion that there is no other way than to turn the dogs around; like a sheer cliff, deep open water, an advancing avalanche or charging herd of wooly mammoths. In fact, every time I get charged by wooly mammoths I turn the team around! I never want the dogs to initiate this maneuver however, command or no, so just before the lead mammoth arrives, I reluctantly go up to the leaders and turn them around by hand so it never happens on the dogs' own initiative. Of course, those of you who regularly turn your dogs around by hand already know that they anticipate the turn, and every time you go up to your leaders you are worried about them dashing past you for home as soon as they see you coming up alongside the team.

One of the more memorable of my rare emergency turns took place in the fall with 20 dogs on the four-wheeler. We were plowing through a deep muddy swamp, when the four-wheeler jammed against some immovable object submerged in the mud and stopped me dead. No amount of heave-ho on the part of the dogs or myself would budge the four-wheeler. Worse, the more we tried, the deeper she sank, until just about all you could see was the gas tank on up. And worst of all, the mosquitoes were draining me at about a pint a minute.

I had a long line on the four-wheeler for emergencies, and recalling my commercial fishing days, I rigged the team, still facing forward, to the back of the four-wheeler. I got to the leaders who were standing in sticky mud up to their bellies, and somehow I managed to slog in a big arc and swing that 20 dog team around until I had them facing the other direction, now hitched to the back of the four-wheeler. Well, after we let out a lot of barking, a few choice words, and another pint of blood, the wheeler started to ease out backwards. Little by little the team hauled that machine, nearly buried as it was, out onto relatively solid ground. I was pretty pumped about the whole thing; the power of the dogs and how clever I was to hook the dogs to the back like that.

Then suddenly I realized the predicament I was in. There was nothing anywhere near us out in the middle of the swamp to tie the team off to, so commercial fisherman or not, I could see no practical way to get the four-wheeler turned around and get the team hooked to the front of it again. Well, since we were less than two miles from home, I thought I'd just drive them home hooked up to the back as they were. Why not? So here I go, just a-cruising along backwards down the trail. It wasn't bad, but mirrors would have been nice if I had much further to go.

Just before the turn-off, I met the neighbor coming up the trail with a team. "Nice day," says I. I don't know why he looked so confused. And the way I was sitting on the four-wheeler going backwards it was easy to see him after the pass, staring back at me, making faces. I also saw how he narrowly missed crashing into a big aspen tree. I didn't need to be facing backwards to hear what he said next.

"Geesh! All I said was 'nice day,'" I thought.

Well, things got better as I entered the dog yard because I had a cordial if somewhat awkward welcome from a potential sponsor who my wife, Janine, was showing around the place. I just shrugged as she shot a puzzled look my way. My wife is good in these situations; she would know what to say to this guy. I'm not sure what she told him after they left the dog yard, but he accepted the terms of our sponsorship agreement with the stipulation that we use some of the money to fix our four-wheeler, which he for some reason seemed to think, had only one gear.

Special Ed

On a rare occasion you may get a dog that is just too timid to really be forward oriented in the big team setting and you can hook them up by themselves like my boys did with Joe Joe. That doesn't always work the best though, because their pack instinct sometimes makes the pup uneasy when out of proximity with the other dogs. You are going to have to get that dog real comfortable with you, and then maybe you can teach him to run following you. Try first to just run ahead of him alongside the team as you go slowly down the trail. (I have never figured out how to do this by myself so you will need someone to drive the team as you run with the dog). Sometimes that's all it takes for them to get the hang of it. We have tried harnessing the dog to a length of heavy chain and hooking a leash to the top of his harness (not the collar). A chain works real well because there is no chance of it moving forward and hitting the dog in the rear if he stops. You can help him get going by pulling the chain with the leash and the dog will run, following you. Gradually let him start to pull more and more of the load. Once he is pulling the chain, and running behind you, gradually drop back until you are even with his head, then beside him, and eventually behind him. If he keeps on pulling, going forward with you behind him, you are a winner. Praise the dog, and do it daily for a week or so before putting him back in the team. Try him with a small team, maybe only two other dogs who you think will not be threatening for him. Then increase the size of the team, and hope for the best.

You can also try letting the non-pulling or timid pup run loose behind the team if he will follow you. The hope is, he gets used to traveling with the pack and you can hook him in later, but this can also cause a lot of problems for the rest of the team, both when stopped or moving. How much of a distraction do you want "Special Ed" to be to the rest of your dogs?

Build Confidence

Once you have these guys going down the trail, you can begin to increase the distance of the runs. If you harness break pups in the spring, you are going to be limited very soon by warm weather, so try to get them built up gradually to at least five-mile runs. Start at two miles and go up just a mile or so at a time. Do at least two or three runs at each distance with one day off in between runs. If the weather holds you can go a little further but I am no fan of overdoing it with your very young dogs.

The whole exercise now is to build up the confidence of your dogs. I don't mean confidence in you; I mean confidence in themselves. Conditioning isn't that important now. You are just building confidence.

Teach your young dogs that they can do anything. How do you do that? You always set them up to succeed. Don't ever run them so far they can't make it back doing well. If they never go on a run they can't handle, then in the sum of their experience, they will believe they can do anything. I employ a very different approach for a team of hardened veterans who have already been trained, but in the first months of a youngster's training you are forming what this dog is going to think and believe about his job as a sled dog. It's like a child. He is largely formed by an early age. Once you form that invincible attitude in your young dogs, they can do amazing things when they grow up.

This philosophy should guide you until the dog has successfully run the Iditarod for the first time. From birth to the first time under the burled arch at two years old, you are teaching the dog that there is nothing out there, nothing about this mushing thing that he can't handle. Once he is ready to step up and be tested there is almost nothing that can happen to that dog that will change his basic conviction that he is invincible. Even if he gets run 15 hours straight during a race one time, he may be tired, but since his mental attitude is already formed, his reaction is: "Wow, that was kind of strange. What a run! Where's the chow?"

So, get them harness broke in the spring and hopefully get in a few runs up to five miles or so. You'll have to lay them off for the summer because of the heat, except in some areas like coastal Alaska. It is good to keep them going as much as you can, but don't risk overheating them, as the damage can be serious and permanent.

Five:
Training Techniques

Running Hot

We should talk a little about running in hot weather here. I guess the best advice for most situations is "don't do it." That being said, there are ways to beat the seasons a little.

I think sled dogs are generally much more adaptable to heat than we give them credit for. The common thing is for the musher to get all excited in August or September, when the temperature may have dipped below 60 degrees and hook up a team of fat, wooly sled dogs that haven't been run in six months and keenly observe that they sure get hot after a couple of miles. They may also keenly observe that their dogs look like they are going to keel over by the time they get home so they panic and swear to never run them in the summer again.

We have learned at our operation that it makes a huge difference if you just keep on running them though the spring and into the summer, so they acclimate to the warmer temperatures. We can run our summer tour dogs with no problem for two miles, working hard, at temperatures up to 75 degrees F. I repeat two miles, no further. It is noteworthy, that 50 degrees, windy and rainy is much more common summer weather on the coast of the Gulf of Alaska, than 75 degrees.

Hydration is a key and some dogs may not naturally drink enough clear water to operate in warmer weather, so give them a tasty broth when they are hungry at feeding time to "force" them to hydrate a little better. And keep them brushed out so they have a minimum of hair on them.

In fall training I want to start going five miles and more. I won't run that far if it's over 50 degrees, even if it's windy. And my dogs aren't real furry either. For us that simply means I run at night or early morning when the temperatures are lower.

If a dog gets hot and starts really panting hard, with his throat open and air going in and out with a decided wheezing or whistling sound, well partner, you're going to be sitting a spell. You have to let that dog cool down and start panting and breathing normally before you go again. It may be frustrating too, because the rest of the dogs may not be as hot and could be yelling and jumping to go. You still have to cool your hot dog down or you put him in danger. If you are running at temps below 50 degrees they will probably go over two miles straight before this happens. It may take you three times as long to get home once they are all heated up, because of the cool-down stops.

In warm temperatures I try to stop for a couple of minutes every half-mile or so right from the start, to prevent anyone from overheating. It probably cuts down on the overall stopped time compared to nursing them home after they get real hot.

The best way is to run in the coolest weather possible. Try to run in the open if it's windy and in the trees if it's sunny. Run through water if you can. This makes a huge difference. Stop and let them lay right down in the water. I worry a little about them drinking too much water, but they don't seem to have any problem bailing out the excess if that happens. Take rest stops on the hilltops if it is windy and in the bottoms if it isn't, as cooler air settles into the hollows.

Some dogs are more resistant to heat than others. Genetics is a big part of it, though nutrition, hydration, and conditioning are important too. You may have heard it said that darker colored or heavier coated dogs are more susceptible to overheating but I'm pretty sure, everything else being equal, body mass has more to do with it than color or coat. I also know that certain lines run better in the heat, and coat doesn't seem to play much of a part. Anyway, in the summer you have to be careful with all of them, and keep them cool. Again, run in the coolest part of the day, stay on shaded trails, and run through water if you can.

Overall, the conditioning gained from running when it's too warm isn't worth risking overheating, and if you do get one too hot he may be harmed physically, and just as seriously, he may decide he doesn't like it much.

Training in Earnest

Once the weather cools in the fall you can begin training in earnest. You will have to start out with short runs of about four or five miles and build up very gradually. This keeps them happy and positive, again building confidence that they can always handle the run. Here is an approximate schedule you can follow, and it works real well if you do it right.

October 1-15	4-5 mile runs, every other day
October 15-31	build up gradually to 10 miles, every other day

Training Techniques

November 1-15	build up gradually to 15 miles, every other day
November 15-30	build up gradually to 20 miles, every other day
December (all month)	20-mile runs, every other day – take a week off for Christmas
January (all month)	30-mile runs, every other day (run a 200-mile race late in the month if you can, in 35-mile segments, with 4-6 hour breaks.)
February 1-15	40-mile runs, one day on, two days off
February 15-28	10 to 20-mile run every day until race day. Food drop or mushers meetings are the only days off.

Now, as you look at that schedule you may think we are training a sprint team because there are so many short runs. Well, let's consider a few things here. First, this is for a team of young dogs who have outstanding physical ability, and you are planning to finish the Iditarod in about 13 days, just in time for the finishing banquet, not in nine days to win. Secondly, the goal is to get all of your best young dogs to the Iditarod, not see how many miles you can pile on. This schedule is designed to prepare the dogs for the first part of the Iditarod, which will prepare them for the middle part, which will prepare them for the end. Remember they graduate from school as they finish their first Iditarod Race, not when they start it.

This is the point at which you as a musher have to develop some resolve. If you are intending to be competitive in the Iditarod someday, if that is your goal, then get that focus in your mind right away. You may be able to be pretty good in mid-distance also, if you have amazing athletes, but I believe the Iditarod still has to be the focus. Do things right for that race and let the other races fall where they may. If you train a 300-mile race team, you will be pretty disappointed by the time you get 400 miles into the Iditarod. Yes, it seems like the best teams are at the top of the mid-distance as well as the long distance races, but I believe it's because of the level of the athletes in the teams. Those top teams are still training primarily for the Iditarod. Let's put it another way. A new guy has a lot better chance of beating the current top crop in a 300-mile race than he has of beating them in the Iditarod. But if you are the guy that beats them in a mid-distance race, so what? You will be a big shot for a week at the end of January, but by the middle of March you will be agonizing over your dismal Iditarod Race. It can be a long summer, take it from me.

Look, I probably shouldn't even put this in print but I can't think of a way to get you to actually do the right thing unless you understand why. You see, the Iditarod is a pretty slow race. At first everyone is full of vim and vigor and goes too fast, and even that is only about 12 mph, really. Pretty soon it's 10 mph. When it really starts to get tough, and the race is being decided, it's about 9 mph. The leaders hold on to win at 8 mph or less and the guys chasing can't get over about 7 mph at the end. That's it. The Iditarod is decided at 7-9 mph. That's for the best teams. The rest are going even slower unless they are resting so much they are out of reach of the front pack. If you are training an Iditarod team, you don't need to go over 10 miles per hour.

As you go to the stat sheets to check my facts here on the speed of the teams, remember, most of the published distances between checkpoints are exaggerated, so the speeds appear faster than they really are. My sons have traveled the trail by wide-track snow machine in a media capacity and have noted the actual mileages. The total is pretty close to the symbolic 1049, not the advertised 1160.

Training Techniques

Others have noted the mileages, I am sure, by illegal use of GPS during the race, so they can probably verify this fact.

In the 2008 Iditarod, some teams were equipped with experimental satellite tracking devices and preliminary indications show the trail less than 1000 miles in length. In 2009 the hope is to measure the trail with a tracker emitting much more frequent signals, say every 30 seconds rather than every 15 minutes and get an accurate reading of the distance.

I'll go through the schedule and give you some suggestions for each phase of the training, but in general, for the first season, do not go over 10 mph in training. There is one exception we will mention later. That's it. Never go over 10 mph. I don't mean average either. I mean 10 mph speed limit. Not to exceed. Got it? You will develop confidence and speed into your team without injuring them, and the following year you will have a faster team for it.

On the four-wheeler in fall training you can obviously control the speed. On sleds you will need a big ol' drag mat with spikes and you'll need to know how to use it. The smaller the teams you drive the easier they are to control, but as time goes by, they will learn that you will not allow them to go over 10 mph and get better at pacing themselves. I use a different technique for the older dogs, but all of my young dogs are brought up this way. At any rate, you will spend hours and days on the drag mat wondering if this is really the right way to do it. You will see powerful teams fly by you on the training trail, the driver shaking his head and clucking his tongue at you in pity as he roars by. That's okay. Just take it easy and get your best, most talented young dogs to the starting line. Keep your eye on the prize. The finish line is in Nome.

I bet you won't follow this advice. You will want to go too fast. You will damage your young champions. You will see attitude problems that will turn out to actually stem from physical injuries. You will miss training because of injuries. You will discard good dogs whose confidence has been blown by the speed and stress. You will not have enough sound dogs for the race in March, or if you do, they will not be the ones you would have preferred to run. You will fool yourself into believing they are sound when they aren't, and start the race with them anyway. You will end up sitting half way through the race with eight dogs left, and 500 miles to go. You will have a miserable time because you will be afraid the rest of the way that you aren't even going to make it to Nome. You will have some outstanding dogs that will be plagued with injuries the rest of their life and their career will be compromised because they were run too fast and hard when they were young. Even knowing all of that you will not have the discipline to actually train the animals for the event you are entering, which is decided at 7-9 mph. I'll bet you on this.

How do I know all this stuff will happen? Let's just say I learned it through the experiences of someone close to me. Very close.

Fall Training

You should do your summer and fall training with a 300 cc sized four-wheeler. You want a manual shift with five forward gears. Bigger is probably too hard to pull in the manner I am going to outline, and smaller doesn't allow enough control for a larger team. All of the power is provided by the dogs and never by the engine, except occasionally when you have to goose it to get around a corner safely. My pup teams are trained on a 300 cc four-wheeler in 12-16 dog teams. My race team trains on a 400 cc in 18-22 dog teams, but I don't recommend that, at least not to my friends.

The trails around our place are either mud and dirt or swamps. Perfect for fall training. You may not be able to do a lot of training before snow falls if you are confined to gravel roads, because of foot problems. Depends on the type of gravel, I guess. You can bootie for dirt runs. One road I occasionally use burns up a set of booties in 12 miles, so that is an option, but not an attractive one. On those runs I hook the dogs to a Toyota pickup, and just drive along at 10 mph. These runs are usually 20 miles or more, and while the dogs can pull the truck unassisted for a while, I prefer not to have them pull so hard at this stage.

The Toyota has its advantages, such as the radio and coffee cup holder, but it's hard to really tell how hard the dogs are working, and it's taxing when you have to roll down the window to talk to the dogs! I use up to 24 dogs on these runs with the main racing crew but I wouldn't want a pup team to run that many at once.

It's also important to use as many different trails as possible to combat a very real foe to your training success—boredom. A team that appears generally sour and unexcited may just need a change of scenery.

So, put your four-wheeler in your runway, put it in first gear, lock the brakes, tie it off to a tree or other object with a similar aversion to moving, hook up your 16 dogs, untie and let off the brakes, and go. Nope, don't even start the motor. You may want to take a handler with you if you aren't confident in your leaders, so that may provide enough weight and traction to allow the wheels to turn against the motor. Or not. For some serious sections of the run you may be just dragging the rear tires. The engine compression is your brake, and you will probably end up traveling about 4 mph.

This type of run will obviously build up all kinds of strength. It is slow enough so everyone can keep up, even if they get hot or tired, but best of all, you can see who really wants to be a sled dog. Which dogs will pull so hard their chest is nearly on the ground and their breath comes out in a whistle? Who simply will not allow that dang four-wheeler to stop, no matter what? That's the dog that has a chance of making my team. That's the dog I want to invest a year of work in with the puppy team.

Keep the motor off for about seven runs until you increase the distance to six or seven miles. Then you can run the motor but still leave the machine in first gear. It will be easier to pull but the run will be longer. You will want to take the four-wheeler for a fast ride between training runs to clean out the carbon, or whatever it is that builds up in whichever place it builds up in (if you know what I mean). After a few of these motor-off runs the engine will barely run, and if it tries to it sounds like you wish it wouldn't. So when you finish your five-mile runs you can start running with the motor on, but no throttle. Just idle it to keep it out of the repair shop.

From here on out you will basically go up a gear each time you increase the distance on the schedule I outlined. As the speed increases, the team should transition from hauling a load to a traveling gait, but still pulling. Don't be afraid to stop and let them catch their breath. Later you won't stop so much but with the warmer temperatures, harder pulling, lack of conditioning, and lack of confidence, there is nothing wrong with stopping a young team as often as every half-mile in fall training.

Hill Training

I have always trained dogs in relatively hilly areas and I don't know how you would do it without hills. Some of the most important training and conditioning situations are to be found on hilly trails.

As you start out on your four-wheeler training in first gear, motor off, you will find it hard to believe that 16 dogs can even pull the machine. Then you will come to the first hill and you will think surely I should use the motor here; no way are they going to make it to the top. Well, perhaps not, but then maybe you need different dogs. If you could drive your truck up the hill in four-wheel-drive, then the 16-dog team should be able to pull a 300 cc four-wheeler up it. Make them pull it up there, step by step, creeping up the hill, until you level out and speed up. You will be amazed at what they can do, and the confidence both you and they gain from this simple exercise will be invaluable. Stop at the top the first few times and encourage them so they know that's what you want. You are teaching the dogs that there is no obstacle or situation that arises, no circumstance under which they are allowed to stop pulling forward. You are teaching them no matter how hard it is or how slow it becomes, to never allow the sled (four-wheeler) to stop. This same lesson will apply no matter what the obstacle is: ice, snowdrifts, no trail, deep water, whiteout, brush, fatigue, or anything else.

"Never allow this thing to stop until I say 'whoa.'"

One thing's for sure, there won't be any quitters in a team trained like this. You never have to worry about this type of team laying down on you, or refusing to leave a checkpoint in a race.

Now, as with most rules, even the "never-help-them-with-the-motor" rule has one exception. If your chosen hill is just plain too freaking steep, and they honestly can't, in spite of their best efforts, get you to the top without stopping, then you have to be speedy about firing up the motor and give them just a tiny bit of throttle. Just enough so it doesn't stop. Not enough to speed up, mind you, just enough so they don't stop. Better yet, jump off and run beside the machine so they don't associate the sound of the motor with easier pulling. It may give you a better appreciation of your dogs' athletic ability too, but if you are a klutz who is likely to run yourself over with your own four-wheeler then stay on and use the motor. Either way, you don't want them to think what you are asking is impossible, just because, well, it is. That will really work against their confidence. Now just because I gave you an inch on this, don't go taking a mile. Use just a tiny bit of motor, only if they are about to stop, nothing more.

Another thing. Never, ever, ever, stop part way up a hill, even with experienced dogs. Even if you drop your last pack of cigarettes, don't stop until you get to the top of the hill. You would be amazed at what a dog will translate as a "whoa" command on a steep uphill in deep snow, for example. If you stop part way up it teaches them that it is okay to, (you guessed it), stop part way up. Not good.

By the way, never go back to get your smokes unless you can tie the team off securely to a tree. Though I don't smoke, I always carry a long rope for similar situations. You may have to go a ways to find a suitable tree close to the trail.

Obviously, the higher the gear the faster you will go both up and down hill, so they will be conditioning for higher speed as the fall season goes on. On the downhill side of the hills, just let them go as fast as the four-wheeler will go in first gear, or whatever gear you are in at a given phase, up to 10 mph.

Later, when you are running in fourth and fifth gear, you will want to hit 18 mph once each run. This is the only exception to the 10 mph speed limit for pups. Get on a good stretch of level trail and goose it up to 18 for about a quarter-mile, preferably near the end of the run. You want to see who has the natural athletic ability and mental fortitude to run that fast in harness and not try to quit. If a dog won't at least keep trying and going forward at 18 mph for a quarter-mile, if that dog is trying to quit or is looking for the exits so to speak, that dog will crack under pressure sooner or later. Speed isn't the main issue here. It's guts.

Training Techniques

It is hard and a little scary to run that fast, especially when they are tired. I don't want a dog in my team that refuses to be forward oriented if the conditions get a little hard or scary. Don't overdo this either. You're not a sprint team, so speed is not nearly as important as toughness.

This whole hill training thing will obviously be difficult. After a few of these runs you will probably see a couple of your dogs aren't cut out for this. That's really one of the goals of this portion of pup training. It will keep you from spending all winter working with a dog that belongs somewhere else. You can test their mettle early and often on the hills with the four-wheeler.

Six:
Discipline and Negative Training

There are actually very few situations where a great sled dog needs to be trained negatively but it seems impossible to talk about hill training without touching on the topic. There is a distinction between the overall disciplined and well-trained bearing of a good dog team, and the type of discipline or negative training we are addressing here. Hill training is fantastic for producing tough and reliable dogs and it also produces situations where negative training is necessary.

For this section I have barred the doors and increased my insurance coverage. There is no limit to the people out there who somehow think dogs are just like humans, and therefore should be treated like royalty. To watch them with their dogs, the dogs are actually dominant over the owners. Even dog trainers defy logic and nature and try to train dogs with an all-positive approach. Maybe you can condition a simple response in a single dog, but you can't build a reliable relationship with a gang of primitive dogs without order and discipline and a little of the fear of the

Big Dog. Nothing in their ancient life stream has prepared a dog to exist without requirements or a dominant leader. We aren't asking our dogs to simply roll over or walk on a leash. We have to be able to communicate to a dog in a negative way when something is undesirable, the same as we communicate positively when something is desirable. This has to be done with a firmness and consistency that will work in harmony with the dog's natural instincts and produce a dog team that will run 1000 miles in under two weeks.

I am making the assumption for the following sections that you have acquired real sled dogs through methods similar to what has been outlined earlier. If you have, then your dogs will all possess a natural urge to run with the pack. They will travel down the trail. This is absolutely necessary for a sled dog. If you are messing around with a pet dog like your Lab, or the neighbor's Basset Hound, don't expect too much. He may run or he may not, and negative discipline isn't the answer for a dog who simply doesn't possess the natural need to travel down the trail with the pack. Even some dogs that look like some sort of husky may be in about the same boat as the Basset when it comes to natural traveling instincts. If the dog doesn't already have that instinct he probably won't ever make a sled dog much less a competitive long distance racer. This is no place for physical discipline.

Here are a few situations where negative training may become an issue.

Situation 1: Dog runs but won't pull, especially when it's difficult.

We will assume for the moment that you are using a harness and gang line system that isn't hindering or causing discomfort to the dog when he leans forward and pulls. That is a weak assumption, based on my observation of much of the gear out there, but I'll give you the benefit of the doubt. This is a dog that almost right away has decided that he wants to run along, but sees no reason to actually pull, or pulls only when it's easy.

This dog hasn't yet drawn the connection between traveling and pulling, but you may be able to teach him. First try putting him in another position in the team and see if he is better. Try switching him forward and back, and from left to right side or vice versa. This will often work and you will find a position where he will pull. Eventually the dog may be comfortable running in more positions as he gains experience.

Another way to help associate pulling with traveling is to make the team pull-start the four-wheeler from every stop, requiring all the dogs to pull hard just to get moving. The problem here is your non-puller is probably screaming his fool head off and slamming into the harness the whole time you are stopped, only to settle into a relaxed slack-line jog once the team is moving. Grrrr!

This dog is probably also running with his head high and looking around. He is not very forward oriented, and some of the theories in the previous chapter may apply. If nothing else works you could give him one last chance, but it's a long shot. Call his name and a command, like "hike up." When he doesn't respond, stop, go up to the dog, pull back on his tug line, and with a pre-selected willow stick about ½ inch in diameter and three feet long, give him a good whack on the butt as you repeat the command. You have to whack him good, too. Don't just hit the tug line or something. If you are going to bother with this, it's got to sting. You want the dog to jump forward, actually obeying the command to "hike up."

You have now associated the forward pulling motion with a voice command, and a clear example of the "or else"

Discipline and Negative Training

you are packing. Execute this whole maneuver in a calm but firm manner. Give the energy you want to project to your team regularly with the "hike up" command. Be calm and firm, not hysterical and out of control. You may have to repeat this again but don't bother doing it more than a couple of times on a run and no more than two runs in a row. If he doesn't get it by then, get a different dog. You won't make a champion out of this kind of dog.

It isn't worth any more negative training because of the demoralizing effect on the rest of the dogs. The other dogs in the team, who are working their little hearts out for you, are being negatively affected by all this fuss over one dog who doesn't want to do his share.

A little dog psychology may be in order here, by way of explanation, since I'm sure I have riled up some folks by now who would have otherwise liked me okay if I had just kept my mouth shut. Well, as I said before, we have to view this from the dog world, not the human world. When I tell you to "get a different dog" if you can't persuade a non-puller to work, here's what's happening. In a natural pack the stronger ones will not stop running and miss their meal just to wait for the weaker one. He will be left behind. This is what is normal to these dogs. It's what is expected. Anything else is confusing and irritating to the ones who are getting it done. Like the members of a wild pack, your team members are responsible to pull their own weight (pun intended) or drop out. It's called natural selection, and it's only natural.

In the human world we work in a completely opposite fashion because we are ruled by emotions, at least where our pets are concerned, and not by nature or logic or what actually produces the best result. I'm not saying it's wrong for us, but we are emotional; the natural world is practical. Humans divert a huge amount of resources away from success and invest it in failure. Nature can't afford such a luxury.

So, I wouldn't advise investing your time and resources in a dog that doesn't want to do the job. My way
is to work with the dog's natural, forward-oriented inclinations to run and pull, and mostly I just go along for the
ride. I really don't use the stick method much. It is pretty
effective for an otherwise honest dog who may goof off
once in a while, but I don't think it is really worth it with
a dog who isn't a natural sled dog with an inborn need to
run with the team. I'd rather just get a different dog who
really wants to do it.

Situation 2: Dog works but quits pulling before the run is over.

The obvious answer is that the dog got tired. Perhaps
he overworked at first and needs to learn to pace himself.
Some dogs will over-do it a couple of times (or a lot of
times), just going crazy pulling for a few miles, then finish
the run slacking and practically tripping on their tongue. If
you are lucky your dog will spend the night lamenting his
foolishness, and vow to have a more sensible performance
next time (figuratively speaking of course, since your dog
doesn't possess the ability to regret last time once last time
is over, or contemplate next time until next time is actually
happening). Actually, the concept of pacing themselves is
one of the lessons all of your young dogs need to learn, so
if one of them is slow to get it because of over-exuberance,
it's probably worth a little extra patience.

There is also the possibility that he isn't so much
tired as "tired of it." Some dogs seem to do great as long
as the runs are shorter than some distance determined by
them. As you go over, say 20 miles, you may see a dog or
two start to look a little less than enthused about it. At 40-
mile runs you may see another one call it quits. There is
a definite psychological change in the running motivation

in the team as the length of the runs increases. At first it is exciting and everyone loves to go. But as the training gets harder you find the limitations of certain dogs. It's as if this dog's mind is saying "Hey, this isn't fun anymore." Then its revelation time. Will the dog keep on running even when it's not fun anymore? Better yet to have a team full of dogs who always seem to think it's fun, no matter how far the run. That's what I call an Iditarod team!

There is also a relationship between the attitude and the physical ability. The dog that has the greater physical capacity is going to have a better attitude about pushing the boundaries of physical exertion. The weaker dog will sooner display signs that he doesn't want to do it anymore, all stemming from the fact that it is harder for him.

This is probably not a situation where negative training or physical discipline will help. There is a chance that if the problem is all in the dog's head, you can change his mind with the stick method, but as I mentioned earlier, it's not likely you are going to make a champion out of the dog that lacks the physical or mental ability you are looking for.

Situation 3: Dogfights.

This is a fascinating area of behavior in dogs. We could talk 'til the coffee's all gone about why one dog wants to rip the face off another, whether it is dominance, fear or whatever, but we'll get right to the point here. Whatever it is these dumb animals are fighting over, I'm betting it's the same list of things in one kennel as the next. So why do some drivers have a lot of fights and others don't have any serious fights at all? Because one guy has "nicer" dogs? Maybe. One driver doesn't allow any fighting and punishes aggressive dogs? Partly. One musher neuters all aggressive males. That would slow 'em down, all right.

These are all partial answers but the real answer is the kennel without fighting has a very obvious Big Dog in the pack and nobody fights when he is around. By the way, have I mentioned the Big Dog in my pack is me? Yes, some lines of dogs tend to fight more than others, and if I have to, I am willing to whack on a dog pretty good before I let him rip another dog to shreds. (And then I'll have him neutered!) But the fights in my yard or team rarely actually materialize, at least when I'm around. When a dog bristles or growls, a firm but calm "Hey! Quit!" will usually defuse the situation. And even that rarely happens.

Not only are dogs willing to submit to a strong leader, they desperately need one. The life stream they have inherited is one where the individual is wholly dependent upon the pack for survival, and the pack is dependent upon an order that emanates from a strong leader. Where there is no strong leader, there is confusion and fear. This fear and uncertainty causes the pack members to instinctively sense the need to somehow fill the void at the top. Who's going to be the leader? Growl! Snarl! Bite! Chomp! Etc., etc. Lead, follow or get out of the way.

If you don't provide discipline, rules, consistency, and law and order in your pack, you are not only asking for trouble, you are unfair to your dogs. I feel this is one of the cruelest conditions in which to keep a dog or kennel. Instinctively they feel lost and vulnerable without a strong leader. This is what leads to most fighting and other behavior problems. I know they prefer a little strong discipline from a strong leader to a lot of poochy-smoochy, lovey-dovey bear scat from a pet parent-type who they know instinctively can't be depended upon for leadership in a pinch.

Anyway, back to the practical stuff you were promised when you picked up this book. Females and males won't really fight with each other. Females usually don't

Discipline and Negative Training

fight with each other either, unless in heat. Young males are the most likely to fight with each other, but not with older males. Young pups will fight when overly excited, such as on their first sled run but not really to hurt or dominate each other, more as an outlet for excitement. Puppies in the pens will really go after it sometimes, when playing turns to fighting, and dominance issues surface in the pen pecking order. All of the above can be solved with a little common sense and proper leadership.

Say you are leading a dog through the yard on a leash and he decides to take a bite at another dog as you pass. I would yank him over backwards and right on the ground on his back as I bark out "Quit." Hold the son-of- a-gun there until he quits squirming and scratching at you. If he gets freaked out and tries to bite you, grab him by the upper jaw with the lips curled in over his teeth, and hold him on the ground. Hold him there until he quits fighting you and then, when you decide, stand up as if nothing happened and continue on your way. In about five minutes, lead him past the same dog again and do the same thing again if you have to, but you probably won't have to.

Same deal in the team. If you want to run two dogs together, and they decide to fight, inflict submission as quickly as possible. Some race rules or guidelines attempt to address fighting, but it's a joke! No kicking or hitting, no foul or impolite language, or something like that. Well, it is a joke as far as breaking up a serious fight, but it's not a joke as far as rule enforcement goes! You will get ejected for kicking or hitting a dog in a race, even in a dogfight. So what to do? Get it over with long before the race starts.

If you have to break up a fight by yourself, how else are you going to do it? Yeah, I have heard some of the tricks: Douse them with a bucket of water (yup, just happened to have one here in the ol' parka pocket). Pull the tails (uh, huh, and how do I pull both tails at once in opposite directions by myself?). So I prefer to educate them so to speak, that when I yell "Hey, quit!" they'd better decide to pursue some other more benign activity, pronto. I wade in between the gladiators with a stick or anything handy that will get their attention and use it as seriously as I can, without injuring them. The idea is that whatever flicker of a brainwave they may have that caused this fuss, is now focused on the idea that the Big Dog is here, and we are now submissive to him, regardless of what we were doing five seconds ago. (Uh, is this my tongue in my mouth or yours?)

It's important that you keep your cool here. Don't go overboard and actually hurt your own dog, but they can take quite a bit and not even seem to notice. Most importantly, don't lower yourself to their level. Keep your energy calm as possible and in control. You aren't trying to beat your own dog in a dogfight! You are showing him that there is no need or acceptable reason to fight. However, once a real fight has started, if they don't stop when you yell at them to quit, you have to resort to more direct measures. After all, these are animals who adhere to a strict pack structure and often that structure is determined by physical violence. Yup, as in "who can beat up whom."

Don't even start with me here on the whole Zen, ying-yang, yoga meditation, internal power, calm assertive baloney and salami! You can calmly and assertively lose parts of your body in these situations, if you don't do it right, and you can also lose good dogs. No amount of nice talk or waving cookies over them is going to break up a brawl in a dog team. The dogs won't even notice you there, swaying from side to side, singing Koombayah! And if you ever have a real fight, you may see just how quickly and seriously they can hurt one another, sometimes permanently.

My shot at winning the 2008 Iditarod was ended prematurely when the main leader of what I consider to

Discipline and Negative Training

be the most talented team I ever had, up to that point, was badly chewed up by several other dogs in the team. We were camping at a training location, so the tethering arrangements were less than ideal. While I was away from the dogs for a few minutes, one dog got loose and started a fight. A gang chain broke, and at least five dogs piled on my leader. He managed to survive by getting out of his collar and hiding under the dog truck, though he needed a load of stitches and has never been right since. This wouldn't have happened if I had been there. Not a chance. Because I have established the order, with me firmly entrenched at the top.

If you actually get this done good and proper the first time a fight breaks out, you have not only taught the fighters a lesson, you have taught the whole team a lesson. You have taught them what will happen to them if they fight, right? Sort of, but more importantly you have taught them that you are in charge. No need to fear being attacked by another dog in this team. Everything is under control. No need to worry here. No sir, and most importantly, no need to feel uneasy and vulnerable as if one of us has to step up and lead this pack. Everything is under control and we are all safe and secure. Our survival is not in question as long as we stick with the Big Dog with that ridiculous looking fur ruff around his face!

If the fight happened during a run, after you get the fight stopped you move one of the dogs to another position in the team, right? So, who is it that decides the running positions in this team anyway? I guess it's the dog that fights the most and makes you move him. No? If at all possible I would leave them together and teach them another lesson, if needed. Hook them together again next time, and the next time. You see, I'm an arrogant, stubborn, so-and-so, and I, by gum, will hook my gol-durned dogs where I want them, and they will, by gum, learn to run there, or else! Silly, but a little of that attitude will go a long ways to helping you actually minimize the tendency of your dogs to fight, rather than just temporarily avoiding the issue.

Get this stuff done and over with early in the season on the training trail, so when you go to races all you need is the "Hey, quit!" at the first growl and you will have no issue with the race marshal. Now, if your team breaks out in a brawl in the starting chute in front of hundreds of fans, or in a race checkpoint, let wisdom be the better part of valor. Nobody came to the race to see you rough up your dogs and you will get ejected if you do. Just move them around in the team so they will quit fighting and get out of town. Take it as a lesson in humility and something you need to work on in training. You may still be all right, but it's not a good symptom.

Not all growly-snarly behavior is actually fighting. Sometimes it's more like excited football teammates banging their helmets together while wearing them. (I hasten to add that I have never been on a football team.) Anyway, it can be hard to tell the difference until you get pretty savvy to dog behavior and body language and the like, but sometimes they are so excited they can't seem to help themselves, and really mean no harm.

I hate to even tell you that last bit because some of you will use it as an excuse to ignore the whole thing about stopping dogfights. You are so nicey-nice you think we should "all just get along." You think that your dogs would never fight because they love you and would never do anything to disappoint you. You think your dogs are so loyal to you that they will do anything you ask out of pure love and affection. You would never think of hurting their feelings by using force to break up a fight. You probably think they will behave perfectly and run to Nome and beyond because of their unfaltering devotion to you and you alone.

Sucker.

Right now someone is emotionally declaring to any-one who will listen (probably just themselves) that they are going to do it differently. "My dogs are all rescues so they are extra-committed to me and my dogs and I are going to show the world what true canine-human love can be, by running the Iditarod. I'm not going to say one harsh word to my dogs and I will never, ever use a negative train-ing technique. Probably finish in the top twenty, too. So there!"

Well Princess, let's you and I have a little talk, shall we?

On second thought, you know what? Never mind. You just go ahead and have fun with that, okay? Bye-bye now. Mush on! Happy Trails! Whew! That was close. I almost said something that may have offended someone.

Situation 4: General Obedience

I like my dogs to be fairly obedient, and coopera-tive. I just laugh and put up with eager youngsters who haven't really figured it all out yet, but as the dog matures and becomes part of the main program, I demand a certain level of respect. I really don't care to be dragged over to the female row, for example, when the dog and I both know we are supposed to be heading to the towline for a hookup. I shouldn't have to bodily drag the dog out of the dog box or end up with chain marks around my knees if I approach the dog in the circle to give meds. Many times I have heard myself say, "Hey Knucklehead, you have a human attached to you here, show a little respect."

When it comes to giving pills, putting on booties, harnessing, feeding, putting on foot ointment, or any other musher chore with your dogs you will be glad if you have instilled a little respect so that whatever it is you are trying to do with the dog, he knows you will get your way, so he may as well cooperate from the outset.

Many undesirable behaviors can be corrected with a verbal rebuke and a quick yank on the leash. I usually lead my dogs on a leash rather than directly by the collar with front feet off the ground as some mushers do. The leash provides a great training opportunity, while the direct collar method is a wrestling match. I want the dog to keep all four feet on the ground when I'm around, and certainly none of them on me.

Once the dog has done what you want, without a problem, and is calmly awaiting his next instructions, this is a perfect time to give him a pat on the head or ear rubs. Use affection to reward the behavior and attitude you want, not as a bribe or desperate attempt to get the dog to like you enough to cooperate.

Dogs will never cooperate with you against their will just because you are nice to them. They learn very quickly whether you are willing and able to enforce what you say. A nice pushover is still just a pushover in their eyes. Use firmness to reinforce what you expect from the dog, and use affection to reward the behavior and attitude you wish to perpetuate. Once you have worked with your guys for a while, the vast majority of your interaction with them should be calm, reassuring, and kindly. Occasional firmness will reinforce the boundaries and build their confidence that someone is in control around here so there is no need to worry or try to take charge. This is a comfortable and happy environment for a dog.

Early puppy education: Give them lots of attention.

Jumbo and Forest warm up for their very first run in harness.

Harness breaking pups going very slowly.
Obviously, if I can keep up!

Bring along plenty of help on the first run.

Beginners Sam Deltour and Dries Jacobs four-wheeler training. Both ran the Iditarod with Seavey pup teams in 2008 and finished, Sam with all 16 of his dogs

Fourteen dogs pull the four-wheeler up a hill in first gear with the motor off.

First snowfall of the season at our dog yard in Sterling, Alaska.

*Dallas
Seavey's team
doing basic
off-trail work.*

Dallas' team doing advanced off-trail work.

Dallas's team doing ridiculous off-trail work. Don't try this at home. That's an avalanche chute!

x

Snow machines make good training sleds when you need extra control.

Tread, our 2004 Iditarod Golden Harness Lead Dog.

Payton, my main leader for 2008 including our All Alaska Sweepstakes win.

Buddy the Malemute loves mushing! Dogs can be taught to do almost anything. Dallas Seavey cheers him on.

Mitch Seavey

My wife Janine and me (center standing) with our four sons (left to right) Danny, Conway, Dallas and Tyrell, at Iditarod start. You could do this sport without a lot of support, but I don't know how!

Seven:
Voice Commands

One common question from visitors who haven't yet seen a dog team hooked up is, "How do you make them go?" Their assumption is that the dogs probably don't want to go unless they have to, or they are trained like trick dogs to respond to some command like, "Mush!"

I tell them, "We just untie the rope and say anything." Once they witness the eagerness of the dogs in harness it all comes clear. The dogs run because they want to, or more precisely, because they can't help themselves.

When you hear good drivers giving a verbal command to go it isn't really a command at all, it is more like permission. "All right," or "okay" are common, though the tone of voice can communicate a broad spectrum including amusement or mock exasperation at the eagerness of the dogs.

You also need a command that means to "get with the program." I use "hike-up" as a strong command, usually with the name of the dog who needs to get with the program.

"Hup-hup" is a general encouraging command I use in situations such as if we are slowing down more than I like pulling up a big hill or crossing open water. It means everything's okay; just keep going forward.

"Whoa" is used for stopping. Say it with a drawn-out ending to make it sound different from "no." Say "whoa" every time you stop. No exceptions. In the dog's mind it will associate the command with stopping, but more importantly, it will associate the lack of a command with not stopping. Think about that for a minute. You don't need to constantly tell a team to keep going if that's the understood normal behavior. Stopping, in any and all situations is an anomaly that requires a special command.

"Easy" is a good command for taking it easy over a bad stretch of trail or down a steep hill, though "whoa," and "easy" are really hard to teach to the team, or more precisely, hard to get them to respond to reliably.

"Gee" means right turn, "haw" means left. "Straight ahead" is self-explanatory. These are the directional commands and are actually the easiest to teach to a dog. We'll cover them more when we go into leader training.

You can use any words you want for commands but they should have a clear distinguishable sound so the dogs easily recognize them. Also, consider the consequences of teaching them "unique" commands if another driver tries to drive the dog.

Sled dog verbal commands is definitely an area where less is more. A lesson most new mushers need to learn about verbal commands is to shut up. I see it very simply. If you are yapping all the time they just tune you out. If you are usually quiet, then when you do have something to say, they listen. Sort of like people communication, I guess.

I feel that over-commanding actually communicates uncertainty to your dogs, undermines your position as pack leader, and makes them less inclined to follow your instructions. Same with over-encouragement. I personally can't stomach all the loud, squeaky voiced, cooing and silliness often used by competitive mushers in an attempt to keep the dogs happy and performing well. The dogs may respond by becoming more animated but I question whether they are actually happier, and I am certain they aren't more content and confident about the task at hand. I feel the dogs accurately interpret this display as a lack of confidence on the part of the musher, as if he is almost begging the dogs to remain upbeat and perform well. Could be just me I guess because drivers get good results doing things different from me, and if all that verbal cheerleading is your normal way of relating to your dogs, doing it the same way on the race is probably best. A casual ear rub and a calm "Good boy" get me a tail wag and a look of appreciation, and helps keep the fire lit.

While I'm on it, you should never show anxiety to your team while on the trail. I've been in some serious weather and trail situations over the years and I've learned one important thing. No matter how bad it gets or how worried or scared shirtless you may be, force yourself to remain calm with the dogs. This is a situation where drivers may be tempted to resort to a lot of yelling and panicked shrieking and, well, "panicked shrieking" is not usually a command that is in a good sled dog's repertoire.

Say the trail is obliterated and visibility is down to nothing. What do you want the dogs to do? If you think the trail is off to the right calmly call them to the right: "Tread, gee. Good boy. Straight ahead." If that's not it and your leader drops out of sight in a snowdrift and becomes tangled in the brush, you set your hook as you would on any other stop. Walk casually up the team as if you were checking a bootie on a dog. Give a little encouragement or a couple of pats on the head as you go up the team, but only the same as you would under ideal conditions. Casually untangle the leader, line him out, walk easily back to the sled, and try going haw. You see, in this whole thing you have communicated that you are in control and there is nothing for them to worry about in this situation. I think if you convey panic to your team under very difficult conditions, either through over-encouraging or panicked shrieking, you are at risk of a meltdown.

Teaching Commands

My sister has border collies and my wife and kids and I went over to visit and see a new pup she had, about six months old, I guess. We had coffee and visited for the afternoon and along about evening we got to talking about the dogs and how smart the new pup was. I sort of humored my little sister along, thinking I had some pretty smart dogs myself and besides, what could this dog possibly know at this young age?

Well, she told that dog to fetch up his ducky, and the son-of-a-gun dug around in the toy box and came up with a ducky. She told him to get the dolly. Digs around in the same box and comes out with a dolly. Get the ball. Same thing. In all she told that pup to get about ten different things, and he digs around in this big toy box and brings her the toy. Except one.

"Get the horsy."

That darned dog burned rubber getting around the corner into the bedroom, and we hear a clatter and a ruckus and a loud protest from my niece who was playing in the bedroom. Out comes the dog with a toy horse in his mug. The girl had been playing with the horsy so it wasn't in the box, but that didn't seem to be a problem for this dog.

Well, I must admit I was pretty impressed and if I had any chance of getting an invite to stay for dinner I knew I had better say so, though secretly I concluded that Sis had way too much time on her hands if she had gone to all the work it takes to train a dog to recognize all those toys and retrieve them reliably without mixing them up. Yup, I swallowed my pride and let her know I thought her dog was real impressive, and how good I thought it was that her house was a small one, seeing she had no time for house work left over after all that dog training. It all seemed perfectly complimentary to me but her eyes flashed, her nostrils flared and with hands on her hips she said firmly "Rudy (dog's name was Rudy), go see Danny." Huh?

With only normal conversation and referring to each other by name, but no actual training, that darn dog knew who my son Danny was. He had never seen Danny until about three hours earlier, but now he just trots over and sits down in front of Danny and looks at him.

"I'll be cow-kicked," said I.

"Don't let the door hit you in the back-side on your way out," said she.

I drove home that night mumbling to myself, "Just two commands; gee, haw; gee, haw; gee and freaking haw!"

From the back seat a small child asked, "What did you say, Daddy?"

"Uh, I said, we can go to the playground tomorrow. And uh, play on the see-saw."

"What's a freaking see-saw?"

What that little episode taught me is that border collies are pretty dang smart. It also got me thinking that my dogs are probably smarter than I thought. I mean, if that blithering idiot of an ADHD pup can learn all those toys and learn my son's name just by listening to conversation, how hard can it be to teach a dog "gee" and "haw?" In fact the son-of-a-guns probably already know it. Maybe they're just too humble to let on.

So here's the deal. It isn't hard to teach them commands. The hard part is to teach them that they are responsible to make the action happen that is called for by the command. I think most dogs in a dog team know what "gee" and "haw" mean.

"Hey Gut Pile, ever notice how every time He says 'haw' we end up going left, and every time He says 'gee' we go right?"

"Huh? Couldn't hear you, I was busy sniffing your butt. Who is this? Maggot? Oh yeah, okay, let's see, yeah 'gee' and 'haw,' right and left, yup, even us wheel dogs know that. How does He do that anyway?"

So every time you give a steering command, ol' Gut Pile just stands there waiting for the team to turn. The harder part is training a dog to make the team go the right way, come hell or high water.

The same idea applies to other commands as well so let's see what we have to do to get these dogs to not only know commands but to actually do the thing you are telling them to do. Remember when I was telling you about the concept of forward-oriented dogs? I think you will see that it is a great asset to have forward-oriented dogs as you teach them commands and develop a disciplined team.

"All Right" – Blast Off!

Teach this by simple association. When you take off, just give them the taking-off command. Say anything you want, just be consistent. Ninety-nine percent of the time, you don't even need a taking-off command because they are so eager to go anyway. As soon as there is no restraint, they go. Here again, I have witnessed some interesting taking-off routines that included motions as complex as a major league catcher signaling the pitch, and a verbal recital as sappy as the Lone Ranger and his "High-ho Silver, away!"

The way I take off is pretty simple and straightforward (pun intended). Call the leader's name or tell the team "ready." Then give a one or two word signal that means, "We are going now." Period. I prefer something like "Scar, all right." There's no reason to replicate Santa Clause's "Now dash away, dash away, dash away all," unless your dogs are hard of hearing, or you are hoping for some quality camera time. Or perhaps you are just a little insecure about whether your team will actually leave the checkpoint without a problem. Hmm?

Leaving Checkpoints

Which brings us to leaving checkpoints. (A coincidence of course.) There are plenty of teams out there who have trouble leaving or going through race checkpoints. I've seen ads selling leaders that were supposed to be good at leaving checkpoints. In my opinion, this isn't about having a particular leader with "checkpoint-leaving skills." This is about training your dogs to do whatever you say at any time, no questions asked. It's about assuming a role with your dogs so that they will respect and trust you no matter what. It really doesn't matter what the command is; the attitude is what matters.

If you can't produce your own leader who will leave checkpoints on command, chances are if you bought the one on the website, before long he wouldn't do it either. When I tell old Scarface "all right," there is only one possible thing on God's earth that is going to happen next. Scarface knows it. The other dogs know it. I know it. Off we go, away from anything, past anything, toward anything, into anything, through anything.

"Hup-Hup"

I use this as a going down the trail command, as encouragement or to focus the team to a particular task, or for a little more speed or intensity. Basically it means to keep going forward. I use a casual, sort of bored sing-song tone of voice with this command. There is no abruptness or threat or urgency to it.

I may use this command as we approach a big glare ice section of trail, a particularly steep hill, or deep snow-drifts, just to remind them I'm back there, and that they should just do what they know they are supposed to do.

If I repeat it a couple of times they will speed up, and I can use it to maintain speed at the end of a run without really putting any negative pressure on the team.

Another time for this is when passing a team on the trail. This lets them know I want to pass rather than hang behind the team we just caught. I don't like to follow other teams much, so we either pass or hang back a ways. The "hup-hup" command lets them know we are going to pass by the other team in the same frame of mind as passing by glare ice, a deep snow drift or any other obstacle.

On a more philosophical level, some sort of gentle reminder of my presence with the team is important because I'm supposed to be leading this pack down the trail. Remember Big Dog and all that stuff? Now, that doesn't mean you should blabber all the time. Just when it seems like they are uncertain or falling asleep or something. Now, before you maliciously and falsely accuse your humble author of contradicting himself here, just chalk it up to that concept I introduced earlier about balance. Talk enough to reassure your team that their leader is still with them and is in charge, but not so much they tune you out.

"On-By" (Or Not)

Some people use the command "on-by," for passing another team, which is okay I guess. But in my opinion you are just going forward despite this obstacle, just like any other obstacle, so why use a special command? If it is used calmly and sparingly there probably is little harm in it but the more anxious you get about having to pass a team, and the more you yell a special command for this circumstance, the more erratic your dogs' behavior is likely to become. If they perceive that you are very anxious every time you pass a team they will conclude that you are not in control of the situation. The more you get excited and repeat commands, the less control and confidence you are communicating to the team, so the less inclined they are to follow your directives.

Another time this mistake is made is when meeting a team head-on. Upon spotting an oncoming team some drivers will start yelling "on-by," as loudly as they can.

So, I have a question for you. What else are the dogs going to do? Stop and roll a smoke? Maybe pick up chicks?

"Hey-ya Doll, great booty, uh bootiés. Say, I seem to have a little spare time on my hands see, on account a' da boss, he ain't said I gotta 'on-by' just now, so how's about you and me, we head down to dis little joint I used ta know down by da waterfront? Say, got a light, sh-weethaat?"

Nope. These guys sound like a machine gun with "on-by" ammo and they don't let off the trigger until the pass is made, usually due to the discipline of the other team, or until they get baled up in the brush due to the lack of discipline in their own team. If the pass actually goes well you can hear this guy squealing and sugar-talking those dogs like he just changed clips in the gun and now he lets go a salvo with the "good-dog" ammo until he disappears out of sight and sound.

Unless you yell "on-by" 27 times as you approach every obstacle you ever encounter, and "good-dog" 17 times every time you successfully pass one, you have just taught your team that meeting a team head-on is a big deal and really freaks you out. They will start to wonder if you are really a valid pack leader in this situation. "Hmm, maybe one of us needs to decide what to do here."

So what action are you asking the dogs to do when you give your "on-by" command? Just keep running, right? So why not just keep your mouth shut? If a dog in your team needs a "just keep running" command, how about saying "Hernia, hike-up" or "hup-hup" like you would any other time you want ol' Hernia to "just keep running?"

So let us now interpret the much used and rarely contemplated "on-by" command. What it really means is: "Don't screw up. Don't screw up. Please, don't screw up. Oh, pretty please, don't screw up!"

"Hey-ya Doll, great booty ..."

By the way, "on-by" is actually supposed to be "on the fly," a term to let the driver of a team you are overtaking know you wish to pass while he is moving, as opposed to "trail" which means you want him to yield the trail and stop.

"Hike-Up"

This is a negative command for when a dog isn't doing what you want in the team, like he's not pulling. The term "not pulling" encompasses a wide range of messing around techniques employed by some dogs. Sniffing around, eating too much snow, pestering his neighbor, peeing on the bushes, intentionally getting on the wrong side of the main line, refusing to voluntarily get back on the correct side of the main line, letting his tug line go slack, to name a few. If you intend to have an excellent dog team someday, all of these techniques need to be replaced with forward orientation, either by training the dog you have, or by getting a different dog. Forward-oriented dogs rarely need the "hike-up" command unless they get momentary brain damage and try to chase a squirrel or something.

Voice Commands

Did you notice how easily I used the term "negative command" there? Yup, not a pause or hesitation on my part. I guess this section is dedicated to the animal rights left, left, left, right, lefties ignorantly marching to the cadence of false and emotional propaganda. I mean, I might as well be direct here since nothing I have said so far could possibly offend anyone, right? Well, except pure breed fanciers, veterinarians, pet parents, pug owners, Dalmatians, pure bred dogs, mothers, some mushers and all women. I guess there was that one other wee little part too, that even you might have taken personally but I'm sure you realize I meant well, in spite of how it came across!

"Hike-up" is my "quit-your-screwing-around-you-miserable-excuse-of-a-fur-covered-garbage-disposal-before-I-whack-your-worthless-hiney-so-hard-you-will-need-two-stamps-to-send-back-a-postcard" command. You don't need to memorize all of that perfectly, but you will have a similar command if you are ever successful in racing.

I know, I know, positive, positive, only positive. Well, that may work for teaching a dog to do whatever it takes to get the cookie, but there are things in every animal's existence (well, maybe not pets) that are negative, but must be done to avoid another negative. Wolves running hundreds of miles in subzero temperatures through deep snow when they are tired and hungry, desperately trying to find a meal could probably be classified as a teensy-weensy bit negative. What's the alternative? Another negative. A considerably worse negative, I'd say. Raven bait.

There is on this earth night and day, dark and light, hot and cold, winter and summer, birth and death, love and hate, positive and negative, Lynyrd Skynyrd and Barry Manilow. See what I mean? For-crying-out-loud, the world is not all positive, and animals (real animals) must constantly choose between one negative and another and positive choices rarely come along in tandem! I know this because I would rather take cod liver oil than listen to Manilow, but I can never find the Skynyrd disks once the kids come home for the summer.

So who ever decided that animals should live an all-positive existence or be trained in an all-positive way? And what makes us think the dog is actually deep-down satisfied with our human idea of an "all positive" life?

Distance racing does have its negative moments (gasp!); times when Fluffy would rather not do what I want him to do, like pull the dang sled.

"Fluffy, hike up!"

Fluffy thinks, "No thanks. Actually, I'm a little tired here, and pulling would be a negative experience, so I don't think I would like to pull the sled. No, I definitely don't want to pull the sled right now."

"Fluffy, quit-your-screwing-around-you-miserable-excuse-of-a-fur-covered-garbage-disposal-before-I-whack-your-worthless-hiney-so-hard-you-will-need-two-stamps-to-send-back-a-postcard."

Collect yourself a stick, give the verbal command "hike-up," stop the sled, pull back on Fluffy's tug line, and whack Fluffy's butt. As Fluffy jumps forward (choosing the lesser of two evils as wild canines and all other species, except pets, have done since the beginning of time), repeat the command, "hike-up," and let the tug line go. If Fluffy is truly fluffy, this probably didn't actually hurt too much, and if Fluffy is at all forward oriented and has a brain, he will realize that the Big Dog has spoken, and actually means what he says and is actually perfectly willing and able, without the slightest twinge of guilt or apology, to enforce what he says. The result is that Fluffy will now know what you expect when you say, "hike-up." If Fluffy is worth his kibble, he will continue to pull the sled to a ripe, happy old age, though he may once in a while need to

Voice Commands

be reminded with a sharp "hike-up" command, the meaning of which is now abundantly clear to him.

Notice, this is training, not punishment. You are associating the command "hike-up" with the act of moving forward. There isn't much other way to do it than with a stick as a jump starter. It would be easier if you could just restrict their T.V. privileges and send them to their room, but when I've tried that in the past the dog just became obsessed with text messaging!

Remember, this stuff with a stick should be rare, and should be considered a last resort before giving up on a dog as a sled dog. Also, every time you get after a slacker, you are in some way being unfair to the ones who don't deserve to be around all that negative energy. Keep it to a bare minimum. It has to be taken care of before you get in a race, too. Don't even think about whacking on a dog during a race. If you do, you aren't ready to race. I want you to know too, that the vast majority of the dogs I run in races have never been whacked at all. Ever. No need to. I just wish I could teach them to stop on the "whoa" command!

"Whoa"

The dogs I work with rarely ever need even the "hike-up" command. They are running, pulling machines and the hardest thing in the world to do is to get them to stop on command. In an effort to do that, I say "whoa" every time we do stop. This requires a lot of pressure on the brake and a little luck. I have never had a team that stops reliably on command. That's because I breed and train forward oriented hard-charging fools that don't appreciate anything interfering with their forward progress. You see, the problem here is that the dogs are bred and taught to never, ever let the sled stop and no little voice command is going to be very effective in changing their minds.

I have been able to instill a sort of resignation in them, whereby the rascals will hear the "whoa" command and submit to the inevitable if I have a big enough brake to enforce the stopping command. That's pretty much it on teaching "whoa." If you say it every time you stop they at least know what to expect, and slack off a bit so you can actually stop them with a brake and a snow hook.

I suppose if I made it my life's mission, I could train a team to do anything I want, including stopping on command. I just don't think it's much of a priority when it comes to winning races, and to get a full race team trained that way would be a monumental feat.

"Easy"

"Easy" is a lot like "whoa" when it comes to getting the lunk-heads to respond to it. It's pretty difficult. Usually we are screaming "easy" or "whoa" as we are picking up speed and losing control, like going downhill or crossing ice. The "easy" command, therefore, becomes associated with going faster rather than slowing down.

One fairly effective method is to use the "easy" command when the dogs want to slow down. When you are training in the summer or fall and it's warm, include some puddles or water crossings in your route. The dogs will want to slow down and drink water as you go through. Make it your idea and say "easy" as you go through the water and some of them have slacked off to grab a drink. Maybe you will get lucky and get them to associate this with the "easy" command as you careen down the Happy River Steps on the Iditarod Trail. Good luck with that.

The natural thing is to try to use the brake to teach "easy" and "whoa." The problem is that the added resistance will cause many good dogs to lean forward and pull

Voice Commands

even harder as they refuse to let the sled stop. I'm not sure I want to discourage that altogether. A team that is hard to stop is actually a high-classed problem in my book.

Eight:
Leader Training

The problem you run into with talking about training leaders is that you can't really come up with a method that is ideal for every dog. Some dogs will never really be much of a leader no matter what you do and there are others that will really shine without much special effort by you. Nevertheless, this is probably the most important part of your training or at least the most obvious if you don't do it right. Most any knucklehead will run in the team behind other dogs but there are special qualities in a dog who will make things happen up front.

Here is where it is most important that you have forward oriented dogs. Obviously, the lead dogs have nobody to chase as they go down the trail, so the forward motivation has to come from inside the dog. You can't drive or force them into leading, or if you do, it won't last when the going gets tough or the dog gets tired.

For many years I had the usual one or two good leaders in the kennel and a couple of others who would only run up there if it was sunny and the birds were chirping. As time went by I have gotten my genetics and training methods lined out to where most of them would pass as leaders in some capacity. Of course, no matter how many leaders you have there are still the best two or three and that's what you use to win races, at least at the end. But having forward oriented dogs means you have a lot of leaders. They will go forward down the trail no matter what, whether there is another dog in front of them or not.

In an established operation like mine it's pretty simple to let the experienced leaders train the new ones. Dogs learn from each other very quickly. You don't really need complicated methods to teach leader commands either. I always believe the dogs very quickly learn what the voice commands mean even when they have only run in the team, but the main training challenge is teaching them that when they are in front they are responsible to make the team follow the commands.

I have heard about (and even used) some fairly well thought out methods of training leaders, but over the years I have pretty much done away with the fancy stuff because the best leaders catch on and become great without a lot of special training, and those that don't, won't be great leaders even with a lot of extra work. I suppose this all sort of depends on what you think a great leader is but I have no use for a mediocre leader in front of a race team so I pretty much let the great leaders rise to the top through fairly normal training routines.

I doubt you actually heard what I just said. A real, natural-born leader doesn't take much special training and if he isn't a real, natural-born leader, he probably won't be much of a leader at all when the pressure is on.

Now this will put a twist in your knickers. The best lead dog I ever had didn't get hooked in front of a team until he was five years old and he never had one step of leader training. He happened to also be one of the most out-standing athletes I have ever seen. I'm referring to Tread, my Iditarod "Golden Harness Award" winning leader.

Tread was never one to work too hard in training and usually managed to stay just a step or two ahead of the "hike-up" stick. I never really considered him as a leader because he fooled around too much and I wasn't too smart about leaders back then either. However, every race he ran he did a superb job, worked hard and just never got tired.

On the run to McGrath during the 2001 Iditarod, I was "leader deficient" and, how shall I say, "speed-challenged" maybe? Tread was in the middle of the team chugging along, doing more work than anyone else in the team. It was a true moment of enlightenment for me. If I put that son-of-a-gun in the lead, I wonder what will happen. Wait a second, why should I wonder? He's five years old, and been doing this all his life. He will get up there and keep pulling like he's doing now. Tug line, harness, are there any questions?

So I put him in lead and he just took over. He already knew commands. Of course, he had been hearing them for at least four years, why shouldn't he? And he took charge in front like he had just been waiting for the chance.

Tread did stuff as a leader that nobody else does. We'll just leave that right there. But he won the Iditarod in 2004, took third in 2005, just 41 minutes from another win, and at ten years old he led a puppy team to Nome in 2006. He is one of the "Greats" and not once did he ever have a leader-training course or special run to teach him to be a leader.

You may recall some of my earlier comments about becoming the Big Dog in your team so your dogs depend on and trust you. About breeding only great dogs. About building your dogs' confidence in themselves, training dogs on hills, forward oriented dogs, etc. All this stuff comes into the forefront as you work with leaders.

Selecting Lead Dogs

First of all, I won't mess around with a dog up front if he or she isn't one of the best athletes in the team. I want leaders who can run the legs off the rest of the team if I ask them to, and never get tired themselves. What? Who ever heard of a dog that never gets tired? Well, "never say never," but I have seen some who never really got tired while I was running them, and that's a pretty good indication anyway. So, whatever the standard is, it won't do to have a great command leader who is slower or less athletic than the rest of the team.

After a lot of tough racing I have come to have a great appreciation for any dog with guts enough to stand up late in a race and lead the team down the trail at a good clip. This quality far outweighs the ability to write your name in the snow with a command leader. Command leaders are important too, don't get me wrong, but the dog who will get up and go no matter what is also likely the dog who will work commands with you under tough conditions. You want to make leaders out of dogs who are always ready to go, even when some of the other dogs are thinking about a long break.

Again, the best indicator of a potential leader is forward orientation. He's the dog that always wants to go, not messing around or looking back at you or the other dogs. He spends all of his time in harness literally pointing forward. If the dogs ahead of him let the line go slack he runs right over them. Put that bugger in the front. As you start out it is easiest if you have at least one good leader to get you lined out, but it's not necessary. You will have at least a few really forward oriented young dogs if your breeding is right, and you can put them in front and get started training them as leaders.

A word of advice here: Don't overlook shy or slightly antisocial dogs as leaders. These guys are sometimes all business in lead and they are not likely to veer into a crowd of people at a race. They often become extremely attached and loyal to the person who works with them, as a compensation for their insecurity. You probably don't want to mess with a super-freak who wants to dive under every bush and hide, but again, a little shyness shouldn't disqualify a dog. Forward orientation is the key.

At this point in our discussion of selecting potential lead dogs I face something of a moral dilemma. I am tempted to say something here like: "Females are a little easier to train as leaders, but they are not as tough in the long run." I am also tempted to say something like: "Males are a little harder to train because they are more easily distracted, but once you get them trained they are usually much tougher and it is worth the extra work." In fact, I'd really like to say something like: "Females are less likely to even make a top team, much less lead one."

Of course, I'd never actually come out and make such a sexist, biased statement. It could offend someone or hurt someone's feelings. On the other hand these observations are actually true and could help someone else if I shared them. What a dilemma! Whatever shall I do?

"Dr. Laura, Thank you for taking my call. Am I morally obligated to tell the truth to the new mushers, even if it means I may be attacked by snaggle-toothed feminists wielding brooms with sharpened handles, all with no doubt as to where they would like to park their brooms? But Dr. Laura, a female could be a great leader! I mean out of ten leaders I have had that I would call outstanding, fully two have been female. What? Get my wife on the phone?"

Starting Leaders

Remember the earlier sermon about positive and negative? You know, the one about Lynyrd Skynyrd and Barry Manilow? All you have to do to teach a dog a command is play Skynyrd on the side he is supposed to go to and Manilow on the other. It has worked for me. Oh my! Have I offended yet another segment of the population? Oh well, Manilow fans probably don't run dogs anyway, and besides, they don't scare me half as much as the lady with the pug. Well, just in case somebody out there disagrees with my taste in tunes, we can call it "positive and negative."

Stay, Line Up

Once you hook the young dog in the lead, the first thing you have to do is to teach him to stay. You want your leaders to hold the line out and stay put any time you tell them to. Use the command "stay" for placing a lead dog in a spot and holding the line. I say, "line up" as a reinforcement if the leader has strayed from his "stay" position or if the line is too slack.

I have many times hooked up my leaders in the staging area of a race and walked away, leaving them mere inches from other teams of screaming dogs, running handlers, scurrying race officials, and fans doing you can only guess what. They will stand tight against the line and stay there while the rest of the team is hooked up without anyone holding them. That's what you want.

Hook him up first in single lead. Always connect a neckline between your dog's collar and his harness when he is in single lead so he can't get loose if he backs out of his harness. Pull him up tight in the harness, push his rump forward, and tell him "stay." Now go in front of him and pet him a little and let him know he is doing the right thing. If he turns around and goes back, catch him and cuff him on the nose. Line him back up, push his rump forward, and repeat the command, "stay." Go in front again and pet the dog. Positive in front, negative behind. If he turns around and goes back, negative. While he stays out front pointing forward, positive.

As you do this, have someone else hook up the rest of the team. The first dog or two may be a distraction but as the leader realizes the team is being hooked up and take-off time is near, he (being forward oriented) will likely start to ignore your lessons on staying and holding the line out and begin to strain forward in anticipation of the run, and in so doing, accomplish the very thing you were trying to teach him.

Staying lessons continue throughout the run and after you return to the yard. We assume the dog will run in front as you are moving but on any stop, he must stay. I usually settle for staying out in front and pointing forward, although it's nice if they will hold the line tight enough to keep the others out of trouble as well. Upon return to the yard, have a handler unhook as you keep your leader in front with the same method as before. It doesn't matter that you are now facing into the kennel rather than away. Once you stop and tell him "stay," that's where he is to stay, holding tight against his tug line.

Don't expect miracles here at first. It may take time. Just be happy the little beggar will run in front. Keep him happy, too. Apply just a little negative for going back to visit the swing dogs and a lot of positive for stretching his nose out to you in front. Once the last team dog is unhooked, leave him in lead by himself and walk a few steps behind him. Straddle the towline between your legs so if he gets any dumb ideas like bolting for the feed shed, heat pen or his house, you have him captured and you can get him back into position before he gets too far. The dog will be wondering, "Now, how in the heck did he know I was going to do that, and how did he catch me so quickly?"

Try it again. If you can get him to stand there by himself for even five seconds on the first lesson you have made progress. Give him a big dopey display of affection, put him away, and leave him looking forward to next time.

You are actually teaching him more than how to "stay." Assuming this is a first season dog, he may just now realize for the first time that there is a connection between the strange noises made by the musher and the actions he (the dog) is supposed to do. Hopefully some of this happened in the exercise pen as a puppy but this is certainly another level.

So you get the picture. Manilow (negative) behind, Skynyrd (positive) ahead teaches the dog to line out and stay.

Positive Beginnings

As you start down the trail with a new leader, you want to do everything you can to reinforce his confidence. Often they will run like crazy up there for a half-mile or so, and then suddenly start looking back, running half sideways and almost stopping, as if they just realized they are in the lead. Slow way down and don't let the other dogs run over him. Make him see that if he stops, the whole team stops. Verbally encourage him to keep it up. Usually he will snap right back up there once he sees he has to go in order for the team to go.

If you have to, stop and encourage him just like when you were harness breaking your pups. Be sure you use your "whoa" command. Make him think the stop was planned, not because of anything he did. Let him know he's okay, and try again.

Don't run a young dog up there more than a few miles at a time at first. Let him build up his confidence without starting to dread the pressure of being in front. Encourage him when he does well and set him up to succeed on your runs.

Gee-Haw, Straight Ahead

We will continue to assume you don't have a good leader to teach the new one with so you have to do it yourself. Steering commands are actually very easy to teach if you have the right dog. You need a trail with a few choices to make close to home, or you can set up a course just for teaching commands, but I don't think it has to be elaborate. You can make a bunch of loops and corners in a field or swamp but in my experience, a good forward oriented traveling dog will get bored and tired of it very quickly and want to head for home, or the hills.

My trails at home require several turns to get to the main trail and we have several ways to get there. I like to keep them guessing, so right away the leaders are listening for commands from me for which way we are going. An aggressive, forward oriented dog will pick it up right away. For one thing, if he has run in the team much at all he almost certainly has noticed the voice commands you have used with your other leaders as you make corners. For this reason, always give the verbal command as you make any corner. You will reinforce it to the leaders and teach the other dogs as well. It's not a new concept now, just because he's in front. Just the corners we have to negotiate under normal situations on our trail system seem to be adequate for teaching steering commands.

Again, assuming you have no other leader, the youngster has to figure it out. As you roll up to the corner suppose you want to go to the right. Ten feet before she gets to the corner call her name and give the command. "Peach, gee." If Peach has a clue she may just cut right and you are in business. If she doesn't do it, stop immediately and repeat the command. Usually, even if they are dense as a box of rocks, these forward oriented dogs won't take to standing still so she will try something, anything. If she tries to go straight ahead tell her "No, gee." She may then try the left. "No, gee." Finally, she gets it right simply because she kept trying to go in some direction until you let her go.

Occasionally you get one that will just keep lunging forward and will probably start barking so they can't hear you. If you've got yourself an ignoramus who just doesn't know what to do, set your snow hooks and go up to them on the positive side, that is the side you want them to go toward. Be sure you have two snow hooks set real well and go a couple of steps into the trail you want them to take and call her over to you, repeating the command. As she makes the turn, praise her and get back to the sled and take off as soon as you can. If you are too slow you may look up to see her return to the straight ahead trail just as you are wrestling the second snow hook free, and you will have to repeat the process. At this point you probably will figure out that a smaller team, one snow hook and a handler on the brake could come in handy.

I will mention that the negative side is equally useful but should be reserved for a leader who you are sure understands what you want but is just being obstinate. You may encounter this when you are trying to take a corner away from the dog yard with a tired team, especially if you have taught your team by habit (bad habit) that you always go straight back home. Anyway, "gee" still means *gee* come hell or high water, regardless of your present location, ten-four? Repeat the command and if you don't get the desired result and Balto just keeps aiming for home, approach him on the negative side and drive him into the correct trail. Fix it so he would rather obey the steering command than risk having you come up on the negative side again anytime soon. Often a gruff repeat of the command as you near him and the looming presence of the Big Dog will do the trick. At most you may have to push into the dog with your knees as you invade his space and he ought to get the idea that you are serious. For maximum effect, you may have to pretty much disguise your overflowing joy with the mushing experience at this particular point. It shouldn't be hard to do.

I can recall one particularly glorious day in March and of all things, the Iditarod had just begun and I was in it. We were heading out from Knik and the trail was well marked, but there were a few extra trails to be sorted out. But besides a quick "gee" or "haw" here and there, I was just be-boppin' along feeling good, enjoying the team and the weather and listening to the birds. Well, ravens at least; "caw, caw, caw, caw, caw, caw, caw, caw, caw, caw, caw, caw," said the ravens.

Wait a doggone minute. That isn't a raven. That's another musher trying to make a left turn up ahead. Dang! If I ever sound like that I swear I'll shoot myself. What is his lead dog, deaf? If the dog isn't doing the freakin' turn, what good will it do to keep yelling at him some more? I'll tell you what it's doing. It's teaching him that when he hears "haw," it means that musher is planning to just stand there and keep on yelling for a while. Nothing is going to happen! That's the opposite of training. That's un-training! Why, that's no better than...!

Say your commands maybe two or three times, tops. After a couple of commands and no results the dog is now controlling you rather than you steering him. He is able, by doing practically nothing, to make you raise your voice to near hysteria and do your best imitation of a scavenger bird. Keep your dignity, man! Positive side if the dog is ignorant. Negative side if the dog is obstinate. Get the results, promptly, every time, "Oh, He with the Opposable Thumbs!"

"Straight ahead" is basically the same as steering commands, just say it every time you pass a trail you aren't turning on, or whenever you cross an intersecting trail or road. Use it when your leader pulls a self-lobotomy and peels off on a corner you don't want to take. "No Tumor, straight ahead."

Now, depending how far you want to go with this thing, you can teach a leader to do almost anything. I once saw my dad, Dan Seavey, drive a team over a parked car endwise. That was a leader named Sonny, as I recall. He could swim those dogs through deep, swift flowing water too, without hesitation. He's the best leader trainer I ever saw, bar none.

Saying that brings to mind his best ever lead dog feat. Dad once drove his dog team through a doggy door and into the living room. No kidding.

He had his new leader in front of his team as he ran his dogs to Seward High School where he was a teacher. He was heading down a glare-ice street when a poodle darted across in front of his team and headed for the front door of a house. His leader gave chase, with the team in hot pursuit. Somehow he managed to stop with his sled on the front walk of this particular residence, but at least a dog or two of his team had made it through the doggy door chasing the poodle!

Consistency

One spectacular feat I witnessed was by a leader I had named Vitus. He took the team 30 feet up a near vertical road embankment held in place by rip-rap, boulders approximately four to six feet in diameter. That was actually an accident of sorts. I meant to turn left, away from the road, but my mental dyslexia got me at just that moment and in my best Sergeant Preston voice I thundered "Vitus. Gee!" Then in a Guns and Roses-like whine, I said "Oh, shucks!" or words to that effect. Well, "gee" I had said so "gee" it must be. Old Vitus charged up and around those boulders and the team scrambled up after him using everything but their teeth for traction. I think that son-of-a-gun enjoyed making me climb those rocks behind the sled.

Speaking of "words to that effect," I remember one really crappy, rainy day in the early '80's near Exit Glacier when I was out on the river flats training leaders. Let's just say it wasn't going well. The combination of deep snow, tangled brush, thin ice, very cold water, and obstinate dogs had me pretty well in a tizzy. Now, I try to use dignified language at all times, to the best of my ability. In those days I even had a pretty severe religious bent, so it was to my dismay that I pretty much lost my spirituality altogether, out there on the Resurrection River flats.

Leader Training

As I finally regained the main trail through sheer force of vocal sound waves, I delivered one last sermon entitled "Who Your Mother Is Dog, And Where You Can Spend Eternity," or once again, words to that effect. I had the volume all the way up, too. Abruptly, I nearly collided with the team of fellow musher and great friend, Rick Tarpey. I was sure he had heard a lot of the benediction and I felt obliged to explain and half-apologize. (I rarely apologize all the way.) I mentioned that I felt a little bad about losing my cool with my team, though I didn't repeat any of the earlier passages just in case he hadn't actually heard me.

"That's okay," came his wise response, "Sooner or later, all lead dogs end up with the same name."

I'll never forget how foolish I felt for letting those dogs get me all worked up like that. I am sure I didn't represent a confident pack leader to those dogs that day, especially under those difficult trail conditions, where they could have used a little calm reassurance.

So much for my political aspirations. I just lost the support of the Religious Right. Guess now I'll have to spin this for damage control. To keep it brief, I now see a tremendous difference between spirituality and religion and my experiences with dogs have done a lot to enhance the former and diminish any draw to the latter.

Well, I'm sure there was a point in there somewhere if you want to dig around for it, but one thing is for sure, if you give a dog a command and he doesn't do it and you give up on the idea and do something else, you have really undermined your control of that dog and his potential as a good command leader. You also have a whole team of dogs who know you aren't in control. You have to follow through on your commands. "Gee" is always *gee*, "haw" is always *haw*, no matter what. The worst thing you can do is to give in to a dog who refuses your commands, and let him have his way. Never, ever do that. Even if you break all the rules, lose your voice, and do 100 other things wrong, at least at the end of the day (hopefully sooner) you have to end up going the direction you originally said.

Sometimes wisdom is the better part of valor. If I am on an icy trail with a hot team and a dumb leader and I know I haven't a prayer of stopping quickly to reinforce my command if he misses it, I simply don't give him any. Well, after they are already turning one way or another, I'll give a command like it was my idea, but it won't do to yell "gee" and have them drag me straight ahead 50 yards past the corner before my snowhook snags something. Now what? Lead them around and go back and make another pass at it? Then I may be headed toward the barn and if I didn't get them stopped before, what are my chances now? Of course, there are leaders that will take any command reliably so it should be your goal to have a few around.

Use this sparingly. The vast majority of the time the dog must be listening for marching orders as he approaches every corner. I don't want the dog to get the idea he has decisions to make. He doesn't. All he has to do is listen to me for his next instructions. I'll tell him "gee," "haw," or "straight ahead." If no command, then "straight ahead" is the default setting. Sure, leaders can and do make some good calls on the trail without us telling them what to do, such as avoiding obstacles or whatever, but any dog will do that naturally. I'm talking about decisions such as which trail to take and so forth.

You also have to be consistent in your demeanor. I don't mean you can't change your tone of voice, or even get a little hot under certain conditions, but it has to have a direction and a purpose. Any physical discipline has to have a lesson that the dog can understand clearly and when the correct response is achieved the discipline stops. Your dog has to understand that he is in trouble for some foolishness he tried to pull on you and you aren't going for it. But there has to be a way out, such as doing the right thing, to stop the negative correction whether it is physical or verbal.

If you apply discipline that way, fairly, consistently, and with a way out (doing the right thing), you will actually cause the dog to respect you and like you more than if you are a big softy pleading for acceptance from the team, just praying for an obedient response to a command.

Okay, here's the thing that makes training long distance sled dogs different from almost any other dog training, in my opinion. Much of the time, giving you the desired response has an immediate negative outcome for the dog, such as leaving his straw bed at a checkpoint, going in a direction he doesn't want to go, pulling harder which will make him tired, or going in deep snow or freezing cold open water, which is more difficult than staying on the nice trail. These are all likely to happen to a long distance lead dog. To make him actually want to do these things on your command is a bit more involved than getting a pet to roll over for a drumstick. That's why I talk about the dog's life stream and instincts, the musher's place in the pack structure, and the comfort and security derived from the musher's confident and consistent relationship with his dogs.

Vitus holding the line tight in lead. Vitus ran lead the entire way on my first Iditarod in 1982.

Dog Trains Dog

By far the easiest way to get a potential leader going is to simply hook him up there in lead with another really good leader. Sometimes a "really good leader" for this purpose may not be your best leader for other purposes, but it's a good place to start.

You need a neckline between your leaders for this, for sure. It will force the new leader to go with the older one, no matter what. In fact, I think you need one anytime you have double lead. I know a lot of drivers like to leave that out but I don't like to be without it myself. It is especially important in steering situations. If both leaders are so good you don't need a neckline between them then they will already be going the same way on command and the neckline won't be a problem. If they don't initially go the same way, the neckline makes sure they do. However, if you don't have a neckline and the leaders go in different directions, you end up with one getting towed backwards making a mess out of the front of your team. And he may be the only one headed in the right direction!

One reason given for not using a leader neckline is the leaders have more room to pick their footing on the trail. They can run farther apart if they want to. I would personally rather have them used to running closer together, almost as a unit, just like the other pairs of dogs in the team. That way they're more likely to end up both on the same side of a tree or other obstacle. Maybe that's just because I run dogs where there are lots of trees and obstacles.

Training the young leader beside him can be a challenge for the experienced leader, and if he isn't really tuned in he could end up getting dragged around the yard or all over the trail. I pretty much expect my leaders to be able to take the abuse and do whatever I ask, even with some idiot pup doing a yo-yo imitation on the neckline. "Stay" is still *stay*, "gee" is still *gee* and "haw" is still *haw*, even with this added obstacle. Remember, if one excuse is good enough to abandon ship then the dog will probably come up with others, too.

Anyway, if the older one is having trouble overpowering your new recruit and getting things done on corners and turns, just shorten the new guy's tug line a bit so the expert can get his nose in front and get the turns done. This also gives a possible dominance edge to the good one, because he is running a little ahead of the other one.

The best dog I ever had for training other leaders was a squatty little dark gray-brown female named Sparky, who I bought from the late Ed Borden of Kasilof, Alaska. Besides finishing about half a dozen Iditarods, Sparky was excellent for training other dogs. She was about the shape of a badger. Short, wide, and low to the ground. She used her low center of gravity to advantage, especially when yanking a young leader around. If a turn was called to her side she got low and clawed with all fours until she towed the other dog over. If the turn was called to the side the pup occupied, at first she would dive under the other dog to make the turn, giving the pup an opportunity to display his best acrobatic airborne-barrel-roll-to-flat-on-the-back maneuver as the neck line caught him under the chest and spun him like a horizontal top. Later though, she got tired of all the tangles and fuss it caused so she just lit into him, snarling, and teeth slashing until the pup got himself into the correct trail. Did I mention she had the disposition of a badger as well? She also administered her valuable and unique teaching style anywhere in the team. If the dog beside her dared to run on her side of the centerline more than about a step and a half, he was likely to get a chunk taken out of something he might want later. This is where I learned that it is possible to teach dogs to stay on their own side pretty much all the time, a valuable skill when using my particular style of harness and gangline.

Leader Training

In this type of training, a good time to teach the youngster to stay is after the other dogs are unhooked. Leave him 'til last and get him to stay by himself for at least a few seconds before you unhook him.

This is pretty much how I start leaders these days. If your new leader is a good one you will soon notice him hitting commands on his own, sometimes before his coach gets around to it. You will see him gain confidence and take control. You are well on your way with that leader and you haven't even had to do any special runs.

The next step is to put him up there by himself and fine tune things. This step may not be as automatic as you would think. There are lots of dogs that will look pretty good in double lead and get counted (or sold) as leaders, but they never develop to be worth much up there by themselves. I would call that dog a secondary leader but I wouldn't go so far as to call him a main leader. The best function of a secondary leader, honestly, is to keep the main leader from getting lonesome while he does all the leader work up front. Best, of course, is to have two hot leaders who can do it together, or each by himself, whichever you ask them to do.

Off-Trail Training

Some drivers get into a rut in training and just go out and do the runs, come home and feel good if nothing went wrong. They stay on the same trails they are used to, make the same turns with the same commands every time and don't take a chance of having a problem with the leaders. Some even lead the team around the training trail with a snow machine so nothing can go wrong. Well, it may be true that "if anything can go wrong it will," but where leaders are concerned, I say if nothing can go wrong then you aren't getting any better.

Every training run should have some new challenge and development opportunity for the team. Just use smaller teams as you attempt these new challenges so you are still in control and able to enforce your commands. When it comes to leaders, you have to take them on different trails or do some new loop as often as you can. Keep them guessing. I'm sure part of the problem people have with leaders is they simply never do anything different, so if they suddenly ask their team to do something besides just run down the trail, the dogs simply can't believe they are serious. But if you are always doing some crazy thing or another it's no surprise to the dogs when you ask them to do something out of the ordinary.

Now, if anyone was paying attention earlier when I was going on about the dog's fear of the unknown and removing uncertainty from the dog's life and such, you may be wanting to take me to task on this bit about keeping them guessing. Well, I'm ready for you. What I meant before was you have to provide certainty for the dogs through your leadership, even in uncertain situations. Dogs are ready to tackle anything if they are comfortably organized in a pack with a strong leader. I believe that the stronger their confidence in their pack leader, the more they enjoy challenges and new situations. I'd like to think this is at least part of why my troops seem to love trail breaking and off-trail work.

Start out by simply taking every little side trail or snow machine loop you can find. If you can, get out on a lake that is laced with snow machine tracks. Pick one and follow it. Then take every turn you come to. Start turning off on less defined tracks, even faintly visible ones. Now turn them off the track altogether and run in unbroken snow. Next time take them off the trail onto a frozen swamp or lake where there are no tracks at all. Pick a spot as a target and go to it. Decide ahead of time which side of a particular bush you are going on and get it done. Usually the leaders are really listening in these situations because they don't have any preconceived ideas about where to go.

This type of training takes time and patience. Each run should reinforce the lessons previously learned and introduce some new element which is a little more difficult. Consider it a success if your dog "gets it" just a little more than last time. Don't expect them to learn it all at once. We're not working with geniuses here, but some dogs get it a lot faster than others. Oh, and always end on a positive note with a successful accomplishment, if you can.

My dogs really like this stuff, and nothing is more fun than working your leaders in untracked country, when they are really listening and working well. The joy of successfully working an eager and willing leader off-trail for the afternoon ranks right up there with the "high" of winning races for me! Well, almost.

After doing this regularly all season, many of the tough or scary situations on a race are really not a big deal. Drifted over trails, deep snow, glare ice, and passing teams off the trail are all pretty much another day at the office. How hard is it to keep on doing what we've been doing all season?

Nine:
Good Dog

I hope you have the good sense and good fortune to get at least one really good dog in your team right off the bat. He probably won't make you win races all by himself, but you will at least get an idea of what a really good dog is like. Otherwise you may spend a lot of time messing around with mediocre animals and never really get where you want to go in terms of a building a great team.

Years ago I bought a dog named Orca in a kennel buyout deal. She was a really terrible distance dog in almost every way. She would hardly eat enough to stay alive. Her feet were like tissue. She was scared of everything. She wouldn't sleep or eat on straw. She would only run on the left side. She was afraid of nearly all the other dogs. She bit me. What a mess. But, she would lead, and man, was she fast! Well, at least compared to the dogs I had at the time. I never raced that dog but she was one of the most important dogs I ever had for the development of the team.

The dogs we had back then were pretty slow. Okay, they were really slow. My friend Ed Borden joked about his Iditarod team, "I could just step off and take a leak while we were running down the trail," Ed said. "The dogs would just keep going, and I could catch back up before they got out of sight, if I walked fast." Mine weren't much different. Sometimes as I crept along the trail, I would watch a tree in the distance and I couldn't tell if it looked bigger because I was getting closer, or because it was growing!

Orca taught me that dogs could really move out, even on long runs. You don't have to plod along just because you want to do distance. Never again would I be satisfied with an exclusively trotting team.

Dolphin was a female I bought from Iditarod Champion Martin Buser as a two-year-old. She had run the Iditarod on his pup team but he had never raced her himself. Her performance had been so-so on the race, but Martin told me about a minor vet problem she had during the race and we both agreed she would probably be better next year.

She got off to a slow start in training the next fall but gradually improved and made my Iditarod team. As the race progressed she and I just clicked. Well, what clicked really was her biological clock. She came in heat about half way through the race. My only reliable leader was a male, but with a female in heat behind him, he was no longer reliable or a leader, he was just male. In fact most of the dogs in the team at the time were male and Dolphin became the center of attention. Our forward progress was severely hindered. These guys just never mastered the art of running backward but they were sure trying, with her in heat back there in wheel.

Then I had an idea. I simply put her in front instead of in back. It worked. We went like a pack of mad rats for 500 miles with those boys chasing Dolphin and her trying her best to run away. She had to learn to take steering commands along the way. I know she was still iffy by Unalakleet because we ended up in somebody's dog lot about a half-mile away from the checkpoint. But she figured it out enough to get us into Nome for the first of her seven finishes with me.

More than finishing that race in lead though, she really started to listen to me and it seemed to me (perhaps a flight of fancy here) that she actually wanted to please me and do what I wanted. Not because she had an emotional attachment to me but because she figured out that when the team did what I said things turned out well, and when they had needs I was the one with the solution, such as food, straw, water, etc. Perhaps more than actually figuring it out, she had a strong instinct for loyalty to the pack and following a pack leader.

I have had several others since but Dolphin was the first dog I had that would do virtually anything I asked her to do. Even very difficult things. Storms, deep snow and wind; nothing mattered. She would do anything for me. She was a great dog, and I realized I wanted a whole team like that. Why not? If there is one, there must be more and I wanted 16 (the limit) in my Iditarod team.

By the way, I just told you the most important quality of a distance dog and what really separates the greats from the rest of the breed. Did you catch it a couple of paragraphs ago? It is a strong instinct for loyalty to the pack and following a pack leader (meaning, once again, the musher.)

If Dolphin had been a human she probably would have resented my "making" her go through all of that, right? She would have rebelled, called for my ouster, or gone on strike. Well, obviously she wasn't a human, and rather than being eaten up with anger or resentment as a human might, she reacted like thousands of generations of canines have done before. It never occurred to her that I was "making" her do anything. Running great distances for food is what her ancestors have done for centuries before I ever came along. She saw that at the end of every long run I indeed provided food like a worthy pack leader. She deeply respected that, and our relationship and routines became her belief system. Besides, she really loved red salmon steaks.

Tread is a dog from a Bill Cotter breeding we raised from a pup and may be the best Iditarod dog I have ever run. Where he excelled above Dolphin, for all of her virtues, is Tread did it all and never really got tired, at least in his prime. For him the whole "do the right thing" concept was a given. Not only would he do whatever I asked, he usually knew without being told. He was athletic enough to do it without physical stress, and cavalier enough not to get emotional either. I have driven that dog through anything you have ever heard stories about, and where others have done it and made it and collapsed exhausted on the straw, Tread would do it and still have energy left over. Tread won the Iditarod on his eighth finish, placed third on his ninth finish, and his tenth finish was as coach to a puppy team.

Payton is a younger dog who I think is even better, though he has a ways to go to prove it. He seems to have everything Tread has, he is just faster. Time will tell.

So what makes a really great distance dog? 1) Athleticism: A fast dog that never gets tired. 2) Drive: The desire to run almost forever. 3) Pack loyalty: Uh, I guess this needs a little more explanation.

Pack Loyalty

Here's how this works. Dogs are pack animals. In their life stream, the ones that survived were the pack-loyal individuals. Every pack has a leader. It is a genetically inherited law that dogs, especially primitive breeds like sled dogs, must either follow a pack leader or become one. It is mandatory for survival.

The tougher things get (such as on a difficult long-distance race) the more these dogs feel the need to depend on the pack and especially on a strong leader– you. Their musher becomes the only security they have. That's not because you are such a great guy or gal: It's because the dogs are such amazing animals and they come prepro-grammed that way. The most outstanding distance dogs seem to have a deep instinctive loyalty to the musher. The harder things get, the more determined they become to do what you have taught them or are telling them to do. Instinctively they know that their survival depends on following (pleasing or obeying) their pack leader. Their superior athleticism together with the genetically inherited law of loyalty makes the Alaskan Husky sled dog the most fantastic animal there is. You must never let them down.

Setting up a Team

Now that you have a team all trained up you probably have a pretty good idea where you like to run each dog within the team. Lots of training miles will show you things like that. I like to use different leaders each run but I don't often change them during a run unless one of them has a physical problem or something. I want the leader who starts the run to know he isn't getting out of leading until the run is over. My dad, Dan Seavey likes to put a new leader trainee up there for the homebound leg of a run. The dog now knows where he is going and how far it is, and will run with more confidence on the way home.

Running double lead will usually make the team faster and will be less stressful on most leaders than single lead. Single lead is preferable though, if you have any fancy steering to do, since you only have to convince one dog to do the right thing and he can get it done without some lunk-head hanging off his neck.

Good Dog

Generally, I keep the faster dogs toward the front and ones I want to keep an eye on in the back where I can see them, particularly if it's going to be dark during the run. Try to run each dog on both sides of the line and switch them back and forth. It's nice if the dog will run equally well on either side of the line but some will be better on one side or the other.

Swing dogs (right behind the leaders) are pretty important, too. They are like back-up leaders and you can often train a new dog in front with good swing dogs who will take the turns, even if the dog in lead doesn't get it right. The dogs I run in swing are usually leaders too, but then most of my race dogs are leaders.

People like to talk about wheel dogs (just ahead of the sled) and how they are important for power and maneuvering the sled. Frankly, that's where the weakest or least motivated dogs in the team usually end up. Not only can I keep an eye on them, they aren't likely to overwork themselves like a hard driving dog will in the wheel. I've never noticed any particular problem steering my sled even if the wheel dogs aren't all that spectacular. Assuming you do have real honest workers in the wheel, you should change them to a different position and give them a break now and then. The jolting of the sled and dealing with the towline on rough trails makes it a little tougher on them. If you are using a poorly designed harness and gangline system (like most mushers), don't put tall dogs in the wheel because the downward pressure on their hips is even more of a problem in wheel.

I think it's best if you run each dog in as many different positions in the team as possible. There will be some limitations but you should be able to run most of the dogs in any position once you have been training them for a while. When I set up my team lists for training runs I rarely even look at who is on each list. I just divide the master list in half or run one side of the yard and then the other, knowing there are plenty of leaders, and the rest can just fill in wherever I hook them up. This also lets me see how each dog looks in different positions and helps me decide where I will run them in a race.

Spooks

Sooner or later you will have to deal with a dog that acts scared or antisocial. I think some of these dogs just plain dislike people. They learn to cope, but similar to wild canines, they don't really like you. A lot of petting or attention is not really the answer for a dog like this. Your presence is something that makes him uncomfortable and a lot of petting and in-your-face attention isn't going to change him. It's best to be calm and confident around the dog and don't act any differently toward him than any of the other dogs. Make him adjust over time. Besides, if he actually likes your affection he will take it as approval of the frame of mind he is in at the time and you will actually reinforce his behavior rather than change it!

Some dog owners I know will humiliate themselves to no end trying to be "friends" with an antisocial dog. They crawl around on their knees and talk like they have a bone stuck in their throat, hoping the dog will like them. They hold out treats in their hand as if making an offering to the God of Canine Freaks. Meanwhile the dog thinks they definitely need professional help and is becoming less and less comfortable with their stability level with each encounter. Again, if the dog actually recognizes their strange behavior as affection, and if he for some reason actually likes it, he knows just how to get them to keep doing it. Keep acting freaky.

A lot of kennels have those "special" dogs that "need" special care and attention. The musher talks differently around them. He walks differently around them. He acts differently, and does things in a different order, all the while telling the dog that he will change to accommodate the dog, not the other way around. I have those dogs too, but they are handled just the same as everyone else. Remember, if you are rubbing the cat the wrong way, turn the cat around.

Well, I guess there are two things I will do a little differently. (You see all the rules I have are absolute except for the fine print!) Spend a little extra time just calmly petting the dog next to your antisocial guy. He will see that the other dogs like it so why shouldn't he? Your input into the pack affects each individual, even if it is indirect. Spend some time just sitting on his doghouse with your back to him. He will probably come up to your back on his own and get used to you just being around without anything scary or bad happening. Remember, your attempts to pet him against his will are "scary and bad," so just sit there and maybe talk to him in a conversational tone.

In your best loving voice you could say, "You are such a nice, pretty, stupid, annoying dog. I bet your mother was a warthog. (Lovingly) I just love stupid, annoying dogs that look like warthogs."

He will understand from your tone of voice that everything is okay when you are around. As soon as you stand up to walk away he will probably bark his dang-fool head off at you as if you were a grizzly bear that just somehow appeared in front of his house and he'd better warn the whole state. Resist the urge to strangle him. "Nice doggy. It's okay. Nobody blames you for being dumb as a box of rocks. (Lovingly) I bet your father was a fungus. You know, I've gotten more appreciation from a gillnetted pink salmon. Love, hugs and kisses doggy, nighty-night."

Strange as it may sound, I have had very good success modifying the behavior of such dogs with a little firmness.

I will take the dog's chain and tell him to come, which of course he doesn't do. I just haul him over to me and make him sit there while I check all of his feet or something else he loves equally as much. If he puts up too much of a fuss I just hold him next to me until he gives up. "Okay mutt, you may not like me and that's all right 'cause that makes us just about even in that department, but if you expect food to keep showing up in that dish, there are a few things we're going to get straight right now. This whole pathetic 'I'm too scared to obey' thing is over, got it?"

The dog will probably never actually like you or come bounding over with his tail wagging idiotically, but he will at least learn to submit to what you want when you tell him. Remember who is boss around here. Big Dog. I'm not saying to treat the dog especially rough– no, just the same as the other dogs. The funny thing is, with a little firmness you have given this dog some boundaries and expectations. He will be more comfortable with you than with someone who goes out of their way to be nice all the time without adding any expectations or discipline. Another way to look at it is that the dog may not be scared of you so much as scared of the unknown. Let him know he can count on you to be definite and take away the unknown.

One of my great leaders is like that. His name is Scarface, and in the yard he runs circles in a frantic fit whenever someone (other than me) approaches. As they get closer, he hides behind one side of his house and then the other, darting back and forth at the speed of light. Pain in the neck, he is. I just tell him "Scarface, come here."

Now, what do you suppose he does? Dives into his house and growls? That's what you would probably expect. No, he doesn't do that, but he doesn't exactly come either. He just crouches down on his belly and stays put waiting for me to do whatever I had in mind. Not perfect obedience, I'll admit, but one of the training accomplish-ments I am proud of, nonetheless. Nobody else can get close to this dog without getting mowed over by the dog or his chain as he orbits his house. Well, a couple of my boys can I guess, 'cause they do just like me when it comes to spooks.

The thing about Scarface and others like him is they need the firm hand of a strong pack leader to be comfort-able and confident. No amount of lovey-dovey alone is going to give him the security he needs to be a balanced individual. By the way, I have often caught that scoundrel leaning up against my legs as if he actually likes my pres-ence, but that is mostly in the team and not in the yard. I guess he just wants to make me feel good.

I know someone out there is just busting at the cov-eralls seams to tell me about the dog you "rescued" who was scared out of his mind, who you are sure was abused, who needed vet care, who had a speech impediment, who you cared for and because you are such a fantastic animal trainer, human being and coveralls wearer, he became a leader and a hero and a soul mate, and when he "passed" the angels wept!

Okay. I believe you. I want no argument with a coveralls-wearing speech therapist that talks to angels. I am just a primitive Barbarian posing as a mountain man who just learned to type, who has run sled dogs since just after J.F.K. was in office.

(But I can cross a warthog with a fungus and actually sell the pups.)

One thing I hear too often is when a guy acquires a dog who is shy or acts antisocial, he assumes a former owner has abused the dog. I believe this is very rare and demonstrates both the new owner's inexperience and his need to feel important. It's pretty much silly to assume that if a sled dog acts differently than a Golden Retriever throw-rug dog that he has been abused. It's just as silly to assume all sled dogs will have the same disposition. Many good sled dogs are pretty much adrenaline driven and the slightest thing can set them off. As time goes on, they develop habits that can be pretty hard to break.

It's a little like high-strung horses. No matter how well you treat them, the slightest noise and they go up in the air. Drop your glove and they may just try to fly to the moon using you as a launching pad. I know a little about horses and unless they're ground and frozen and ready for the dog food bucket, my opinion of them ranks right up there with a tooth ache. Well, unless you have some big moose quarters to haul out of the mountains, that is. The key difference between a flighty dog and a flighty horse is the dog is small enough to handle even when he takes leave of his senses and decides to put his back feet in your shirt pockets. Some of these flighty dogs can be improved immensely by correct handling when they are young, and admittedly this doesn't always happen in some kennels, but that isn't the same as accusing a former owner of outright abuse.

One possible reason dogs act flighty around the new guy is because perhaps he isn't providing the structure the dog is used to. He feels vulnerable and leaderless. Ironically, the new owner who is determined to make friends with the new dog through affection alone may be actually making the dog's frightened behavior worse by showing affection without leadership.

Notice your so-called abused dog when you come over to him with a harness. Nine times out of ten he will act like a different dog. He probably forgets all about acting scared. Two things are happening. First, you are proposing something the dog likes. I mean really likes, like "lives for." Second, you are defining for him what is going to happen. Harness up and run. You have removed

Good Dog

the uncertainty and fear of the unknown. On the trail the timid dog will usually act as comfortable as any other dog in the team. He is comfortable. He knows what is happening and it is well within his control. "If I am wearing the harness I know what to do and I can handle this, no problem." At least that's what I think I've observed in my experience with spooks.

Ten:
Care and Feeding of the World's Best Athletes

Feeding Racing Dogs

This is an area where there are as many methods as there are mushers. I, of course, have the best methods of all time. That may be because no matter the method, I have probably tried it at some time. I have had some very complex trail menus for my dogs including things like custom sausages commercially made to my specifications, or "power snacks" made in our kitchen, to the chagrin of handlers and family members. These complex and professionally formulated nutritional wonders have been the delight of ravens and foxes all over the state of Alaska after my pooches left them lay beside the trail.

Over time I have returned to simplicity as a key ingredient of my trail diet for racing dogs. There is some merit to having a little diversity or a couple of surprise treats here or there but mostly the dogs will do best on what they are used to, and if they don't choose to eat it, it's not because there is something wrong with the food.

That brings up an important point in racing dogs. The dogs have to eat well, and you can't really tell about their eating habits until you put them under stress. It would seem like the more you run them the hungrier they should get, so they should eat like starved wolves. Well, it just doesn't work that way. Stress seems to put some dogs into a defensive mode where they don't want to eat, at least not right away after a run. You will see this mostly in actual races and it shouldn't be a big problem in training, but you will want to maximize the eating habits of your dogs at all times. I have heard race officials say that if a race dog doesn't eat he is either sick or exhausted– no further discussion. Well, sometimes there are things on the dog's priority list above food, even when he should be hungry. Just feed an intact male next to an in-heat female and see whether he looks like he has good eating habits. Strange surroundings can put some dogs into a "surveillance" or "sentry" mode depending on their position in the pack, rather than an "eat, drink and be merry" mode. Strangers, notably race officials, approaching up close and personal during a rest stop can trigger a flood of adrenaline in some dogs that will leave their little heart pounding for at least a half-hour, and while in this fight or flight mode eating is the furthest thing from their mind.

This eating habit thing is why I told you to only feed pups once a day and don't ever over-feed your dogs. Make them appreciate feeding time as an event not to be missed, even if the race vet is nearby. Along these lines I keep them eating well at all times, even under stressful training conditions. You don't want them too thin of course, but I believe eating habits are more important than body weight and obviously the way they eat will dramatically affect body weight where it really matters, out on the race trail. If a dog doesn't eat enough during training to keep good weight on without you having to baby him a lot or spoil him rotten, that dog probably shouldn't be a long distance racing dog. If it takes heroics to keep weight on him at home, it may be impossible to keep weight on him on the race trail.

Here is how I feed my racing dogs during training:

Morning broth

Make up some buckets with something in it to flavor the water, like a half a shovel-full of sawdust from your meat saw or maybe a couple of pounds of ground meat and a couple of pounds of ground liver. Variety here is a good idea. Maybe you have time to cook up a little fish to flavor the buckets. The dogs will love it. Add ten cups of high quality dry kibble (I feed and recommend Blackwood 7000), just before you go out and feed it to them. Fill a five-gallon bucket to ¾ full. This will be for 10 –12 dogs. I use a one-quart scoop (ladle) on a long handle to feed with. Give the dogs one to two scoops, depending on the size of the dog. You have to stir a lot before feeding each dog so they get some of everything in the bucket, since it will be mostly water.

This is supposed to be mostly a watering for hydration but if you are about to go do a 50-mile run the calories will help too. Don't overdo the food in this feeding; otherwise you have to wait a long time before you can go run, and it may put a damper on their appetite for their main meal later. With the recipe I just gave you, you can take off in just 1½ hours or so, and I bet you can't actually get ready and leave that fast anyway. I mean I could, of course, but most people…

If you are running 50 or so miles, it is long enough in my oh-so-humble opinion to give the dogs a snack at about half way. On a race, I normally wouldn't snack at all on a 50-mile run but this is an opportunity to teach them how you are going to do snack stops. They are usually pretty good about letting the other guy get his snack and waiting their turn once they see that you intend to give one to everybody. I like to hand the snack to each dog and let him take it out of my hand. That way there isn't much opportunity to fight over the food. It commits the dog to take the snack and once it is in his mouth he is more likely to eat it than if you throw it on the ground and he feels he may have to compete with his neighbor for it. Some dogs don't like to take it out of your hand but will eat it if you drop it in front of them and step back. That's okay with me since it is a type of pack behavior but it means you have to make sure the right dog gets the snack if his neighbor is more aggressive than he is.

Any frozen quarter-pound chunk of meat or fish (not fat) will do for a snack. You can even soak up some dry food and freeze it into cookies for snacks if that is what you have. I don't go for snacking more often than every couple of hours, because it will reduce their appetite for their main meal, even if the amounts fed are smaller. Some people snack religiously every hour and are really happy with the results. I think the results have more to do with stopping every hour than snacking every hour but maybe we should save that topic for another day.

I prefer to feed the dogs as soon as possible after a 50-mile training run. This associates the end of a run with eating and conditions the dogs to expect to be fed right away, as they will be on a race. One exception to this rule is if it is very warm out, say thawing temperatures. Dogs just don't eat as well when it's that warm so I let them sit for a couple of hours to cool down and start feeling hungry. I think that is better than ladling out a bunch of food and giving them the opportunity to turn their nose up at it.

Another exception is if I just don't feel like feeding them right at that particular time. That's reason enough for me. I just don't feel like it.

You surely know by now that your wily author (side-splitting laughter here) usually has a good reason for his off-beat comments. And you'd be right in this case.

Another element to maintaining good eaters is unpredictability. I intentionally try not to be too scheduled about my feeding schedule. Whenever the food comes, whether it's at 5:00 pm right after a run or I wake up in my chair at 1:00 am and go back out to feed, they are happy to see me. But usually it is within an hour after the run.

Evening Feeding

Right after the morning broth you start your buckets for the evening. Put ten pounds of ground meat in each five-gallon bucket for ten dogs. Add two pounds of ground liver unless you already gave it to them with their morning broth. Add about 2½ pounds of ground beef fat or whatever kind of fat you have. There is quite a bit of difference in fats but it probably won't matter much to your team at this phase of their development. (More on fat in a bit.) Add enough hot water to cover the stuff in the bucket and let it thaw all day. Put a lid on it to keep the cat out.

Some people get pretty finicky about dirty buckets and bowls, and bacteria counts in the food, etc., so I probably should defend myself and my unsanitary practice of leaving meat sit around thawing all day.

But I won't.

All I can say is it has never been a problem as far as I know, and I want the dogs to be used to everything they may come into contact with later. It is sort of like when we went to the Caribbean and drank the water. The effects on me were drastic and dramatic, while the locals had no problem at all. Well, I assume they had no problem because they were walking around normally, as opposed to the hunched over waddle of a skinny white boy in flowery shorts, hustling to the outhouse.

Did I just defend myself and my unsanitary practices? I am so embarrassed.

Anyway, when you get ready to feed at night, add 15 cups (1½ #10 cans full) of dry food per five-gallon bucket, any vitamins or other supplements, and perhaps ½ cup of corn oil. Stir it up and fill the buckets the rest of the way with hot water.

Feed 1½ to 2½ scoops per dog with your one-quart ladle. The trick here is to feed them just about all they can eat but stop before they do. You want to avoid feeding them so much that they refuse the last bit. Keep them wanting a little bit more.

If they start slowing down on eating the first thing you do is cut down on the fat or leave it out altogether. You want them to eat at least three quarts of the soupy food a day including the morning broth and the evening meal because that is their main source of water, and as you know, water is the most important "nutrient" in any diet. To that end, I have also skipped the evening meal on a few dogs that decide they don't want their morning broth: "Okay, no more chow for you until you show a little more appreciation for me and this food bucket." At 50 or more miles a day in training, their appetite usually responds very quickly.

Fat is the biggest variable in the diet. When it is warm and the work is minimal, they may not need any added fat at all. But doing long runs in cold weather, they need to get about half or a little more of their calories from fat.

That is 55% of their dietary calories of metabolized energy from fat sources, as a percentage, on a dry matter basis. Remember to factor in the digestibility quotient of the sources used for fats, carbohydrates and proteins, and the relative caloric density of the respective nutrient sources.

What the...! Sorry for that last paragraph, I think I fell asleep at the keyboard there. I'll try again.

Feeding beef fat or something similar, you can add up to a quarter-pound per dog. That's a chunk the size of a stick of butter, or roughly a cup per dog of ground fat. Add a tablespoon of corn oil per dog as well. Reduce or eliminate one or both of those in warm weather or if the dogs get too fat or fussy. When I use seal oil I just substitute it for the corn oil every other day. Don't worry about calories or percentages or whatever. If you stay close to those guidelines you'll do real well. You can always add balanced ingredients like meat, fish, or high quality commercial food in any amount as long as the stools stay fairly small, firm, and dark colored, indicating good digestion. For example, I will increase the commercial food from 1½ cans to 2 cans per bucket when they are really working hard.

Just a word on commercial dry kibble: I started feeding Blackwood 7000 the season before I won the Iditarod in 2004. I decided to switch to it after I did a pretty thorough test of many different foods in our kennel, and I liked it the best. I bought a lot of tons of the stuff before the company began to sponsor us. At any rate, for those of you who think premium foods are too expensive for you to feed, just divide out the cost of the food by the calories provided. You will find that Blackwood and other premium feeds are actually less expensive per calorie provided, besides being more digestible and better for your dogs.

You may have heard it said that you should feed the best food you can afford to your dogs, but I say, only have as many dogs as you can afford to feed the best food.

There is a lot more to feeding during an actual 1000-mile race, but this will get you going in the right direction for the training phase at least.

Cleanup

Now after you feed all of that food to a dog, something is bound to happen. He will probably express his appreciation by depositing last night's food on the ground at your feet. He will probably express his appreciation this way at least a couple of times a day. You must not break the code of sled dog etiquette by leaving his little "present" lying there as if you don't appreciate it. No, in fact you must collect his offering in a bucket at your earliest convenience.

In other words, dogs poop a lot. It's best to clean up at least once a day, better yet, twice a day. After only a few hours you can go through and clean up in a hurry but the longer you let it go the harder it gets, especially if you calculate in the "smear factor."

The smear factor is a complex rating system for the condition of the dog lot facing the cleaning crew each morning. It can be expressed in a number of ways but the settings on your common household blender are useful in many cases. "Puree" may be the appropriate term for the yard if there was a moose grazing in the lawn a matter of mere feet from the yearlings all night. "Frappe" may apply to the male section if there are females in the heat pen. I have heard the "juice" setting referred to after I had run two teams out of the yard early, before cleaning. The blender vocabulary, though useful, may be inadequate for some situations. When my young son, Conway, spends the afternoon next to the dog yard playing a form of baseball with his dog Eagle, (who has a second life as one of the best dogs in my racing team), the condition in the puppy pens the following morning will probably be referred to as "atomized."

Freezing weather adds a new dimension to the yard cleaning vocabulary. Among the words that can be printed here, I have heard of hockey pucks, dilly bars, stalagmites, frozen bananas and walnut veneer mentioned. These frustrated conversations invariably lead to the age-old idea of situating the winter dog lot on a frozen lake and just letting the ice go out in the spring. Bye, bye dilly bars. I rather like the idea myself. I've always wanted to live next to a pond where I could fish in the summer.

Use a small leaf rake about six inches wide with steel tines and an aluminum grain shovel or other square shovel. Just rake the poop onto the shovel and deposit it into the bucket. This works best for summer weather, when the ground and poop isn't frozen. In the winter when you have freezing temperatures and snow, just use a round point shovel and a bucket. Practice makes perfect so don't despair. This is a killer skill on a resume!

It is never a good idea to skip cleaning. It just gets harder later, and after this stuff gets stomped around a while you will never get it all up. We try to get it all up, too. Leave nothing larger than a pea. I suppose I am a bit of a neat freak where this is concerned because I am sure the dogs don't really care too much, but it's about the kind of environment I choose to work in.

Strange as it seems, this can be a really good time in the dog lot with your dogs. They are usually pretty mellow about it because they aren't anticipating feeding or running– just cleaning. You can hang out with the dogs and clean up the yard without a lot of noise and excitement going on. It's a cool atmosphere.

Care and Feeding of the World's Best Athletes

What goes in...

...must come out!

Foot Care

You have to pay pretty close attention to your dogs' feet when you start doing long runs. It's really not much of a problem during fall training on dirt but even then, if you run on a lot of sharp gravel you will have to protect the dogs' feet. Also, frozen ground is pretty unforgiving and never run on pavement, but otherwise summer and fall foot care is minimal. The snow and colder temperatures of winter bring on a new set of challenges in foot care.

First you have to get real familiar with dog booties. These cloth foot protectors are a minor miracle in mushing and without them we really couldn't do the long races like the Iditarod. At least not the way we do it today.

I have heard mushers claim their dogs didn't need booties or they ran the entire Iditarod without booties. I guess it could be true in limited cases, but I'm skeptical, and for all practical purposes you will have to bootie your dogs every run on a thousand-mile race. I am also sure that the harder a dog works the harder it is on his feet, especially his back ones. That's where the rubber hits the road, so to speak. I think dogs get graded unfairly for having either really good or really poor feet, when maybe the amount of stress being put on the feet by the dog's work ethic is a larger part of the question.

Most mushers in the very first Iditarod in 1973 didn't even take booties with them on the trail. My dad took a complete set for his team but no spares, as I recall. They just didn't plan on using them or know that they would need them. It didn't take long for them to realize the error and the call went out all over Alaska for volunteers to make booties to be sent up the trail and handed out to the mushers for their dogs. These booties were made of pillow ticking and were held on with adhesive tape.

Velcro was invented, or became available, in the early '80s and made booting a team of dogs somewhat easier. The system then, invented by 1980 Champion Joe May I believe, involved a Velcro patch on each disposable bootie and a separate reusable Velcro strap to hold the bootie on. The hard part of this was managing a tangled, clingy, basketball-sized wad of eight-inch long Velcro straps with frozen fingers. Sometimes the adhesive tape almost seemed easier.

The booties we have today are really quite good, which is probably why they haven't been modified in a decade or so. They are made out of tough cordura fabric and close with stretchy Velcro which is easy on the dogs' wrists. They are easy to put on and last about 100 miles, depending on the conditions.

Anyway, on a long race you might as well bootie every foot on every run. It will save you time in the long run. There are exceptions once you get competitive, but not too many. In training I generally bootie only the feet that have a problem, unless it is colder than minus 20 F or the texture of the snow or ice on the trail is particularly abrasive. Then I bootie everything.

Booties come in several sizes and you will need to be familiar with the sizing of your chosen brand of booties. Most of my 50-pound males use large booties on the front and medium on the back. A 45-pound dog may use all medium and some will take small on the back. The thing is to use as small a bootie as you can that still allows the toes to spread out naturally as the dog steps down on the foot.

You have to watch the booties for holes. Generally even the tiniest hole in a booty means it's time to throw it away because it will fill up with snow.

You have to check your dogs' feet often during the winter. Look for any type of nick, cut or abrasion. Check the toenails and toes by pushing in (toward the foot) on each toenail and observe any reaction by the dog. Check the bottoms of the feet, between the toes, for what mushers call web splits. Vets refer to the same problem as "interdigital fissures," for some reason. They look like a crack or split in the skin between the toes. Treat it with an antibiotic ointment every day and it should clear up in a week or so. You could end up with this problem on quite a few feet in your team after a long run or if you don't bootie when you should. Don't panic. Young dogs just have to go through this until their feet get tougher. Keep the ointment and booties on and the dog shouldn't have to miss any runs.

If you have a really wimpy dog his performance may be affected even by the smallest foot problem. I personally don't like dogs who let a small web split or two affect their performance. On the other hand, if you don't take care of their feet then that's your fault, and your dogs may get so bad they aren't fit to run, and if you do run them, they may develop other injuries from adjusting their gait to compensate for sore feet.

In persistent cases there is another way to speed up the healing of the splits. Put an antiseptic soap solution in the bottom of an airline kennel, about an inch deep, and let the dog stand in it for about a half-hour a couple of days in a row. Remove any dark scabby buildup and keep the ointment on there. If the dog's foot has gotten infected, beyond just the surface of the splits, you will see swelling and feel heat in the dog's foot and leg, and this won't likely be cured with topical remedies. You will have to put the dog on oral or injectable antibiotics to prevent a potentially fatal systemic infection.

Toenails will probably stay short enough in the summer and fall from running on the dirt and gravel, but on snow, especially if you are using booties a lot, they will get long in a hurry. You'll have to keep those trimmed, about even with the bottom of the pad of the foot. If you cut one too short you'll know. It will bleed like crazy, though the dog probably won't really be bothered at all.

Care and Feeding of the World's Best Athletes

You also need to trim the hair on the bottom of the dogs' feet to prevent ice balls from forming and clinging to the hair. You can use a scissors or an electric clipper and trim it even with the pads. Don't take it out from between the toes though, because dogs without any hair between their pads can form big ice balls in there when running barefoot in snow.

After you've trimmed the hair you need to "candle" their feet, or singe the ends of the hair that you trimmed. This makes snow even less likely to collect in the foot hair.

Notice the term is "candle" the feet. My boys are always looking for faster ways to do their chores. I suppose that is why they started using a propane torch to "candle" dogs' feet. That in turn explains why, upon entering the shop one winter's day, I observed the back half of my best leader apparently going up in flames. This gives a whole new meaning to the term, "Put the dog out, son!"

A lighter works fine, and the torch is okay too, if you have sense enough to keep the flame on some setting lower than "blowtorch."

Use a good foot ointment on every foot, every day during hard training. Algyval is good, and there is other stuff you can use as well, for maintenance of the feet. In addition, use an antibiotic ointment on any cuts or splits. Daily attention to the feet and proper use of booties will prevent anything on the feet from getting out of hand.

Hey now! Don't just brush that last statement aside! Daily attention to the feet means daily, even when you just got home late, or it's thirty below outside. Aren't you just dying to get out there and spend about an hour with your sore back bent over, getting goop all over your bare hands and smearing it between the toes of about a hundred snowy little feet? Okay, that's better. Put down the remote and the beer and get out there and do your dogs' feet. Micro-

159

wave several small containers of ointment and keep spares in your inside pocket so you always have a warm one to work out of as you go through your team. This could be fun! Just pretend you are your favorite Iditarod musher. Hurry now, I'll time you.

The Curse of the Velcro

I would not be doing my readers justice if I failed to expound on what I consider to be one of the most frustrating and potentially dangerous aspects of dog mushing. I mentioned that Velcro came into prominence in the 80's and every clever manufacturer of anything to do with the outdoors or sled dogs has been making liberal use of it ever since. So today I have Velcro on my boots, Velcro on my pants, Velcro on my parka, Velcro on my mitts, Velcro on my hood, Velcro on my hat, and Velcro on my headlight. There is Velcro on my sled bag, Velcro on my handlebar bag, and Velcro on my sleeping bag. My dogs have Velcro on their booties, Velcro on their wrist wraps, Velcro on their male wraps, Velcro on their shoulder coats, and Velcro on their dog jackets. Just about everything that fastens in any way, does so with Velcro. Even my watchband has Velcro.

So what is the problem? I'll explain. You see Velcro is more scientifically known as hook and loop fastener. The problem is that the inventor of Velcro forgot just one little detail. When there is a lot of Velcro around, the hook part doesn't much care which loop part it fastens to. In fact, it doesn't even care if it fastens to Velcro at all. Wool, fleece, dreadlocks, belly-button lint, or just about anything else will do. (This is why you should never wear your mushing parka to bed with your spouse.) Every time a musher tries to thaw the frost off his mustache with his hand, his parka cuff sticks to his hat, and if he pulls his hand away suddenly he may remove his hat, hood, and headlight all at once. Don't worry. Nothing will be lost on the trail. As the stuff falls on the sled bag the hook Velcro on the sled bag flap will undoubtedly grab the loop Velcro on the hat, making for easy retrieval.

Camping can be a nightmare. Imagine a physically exhausted and sleep-deprived musher facing a dog sled full to overflowing with Velcro-infested gear. Every time he ventures his hand into the sled he comes out with more Velcro stuck to him. Soon he is covered in Velcro from head to foot, and as it swarms over him and engulfs him in its clingy grasp, he sinks to the ground in helpless defeat and is soon swallowed up by Velcro! That person is not likely to finish the race but he should not be ashamed, as many good mushers before him have succumbed to the Curse of the Velcro. In my expert opinion that musher should have just given up on getting his thermos out of the sled long before the Velcro overtook him. Just a rookie mistake.

Honestly, I have observed many a tired musher stumbling about the checkpoint with some accessory Velcroed to his person without his knowledge. Experienced dog team campers can usually limit this indignity to a spare booty or two clinging to the vest pocket or a wrist wrap stuck to the suspenders. But during the '03 race, I swear I saw one of those moving and inspirational sights the Iditarod is so famous for. It was a testament to the willpower of the human spirit, a true heart rending scene. I saw a young musher struggling toward the bunkhouse, nearly dragged to the ground and almost subdued; he still had that fire-in-the belly and never-say-die look on his face. It was a look that said he would get inside that bunkhouse and save the family farm, even if his lead dog was injured! His sleeping bag was stuck to his headlight strap. A dog bootie clung to his left eyebrow. His entire sled bag stuck to the

Velcro of his nylon pistol holster (without a gun in it), as he plowed forward one weary step after another, clutching his thermos to his chest with both arms. Only three steps separated him from his goal of a half-hour nap. One, two...two... oh, too bad! He fell unconscious, overcome by the Curse of the Velcro. Even as a heartless Barbarian, I was a little moved by this kid's determination, but hey, this is a competition. I told him to leave the thermos. There's a coffee pot inside. Dumb rookie.

I stepped over his near-freezing body and went inside the checkpoint. At this particular stop I was feeling pretty smug, as I had escaped the Curse of the Velcro almost completely. I had made it inside the checkpoint building with only one dog coat Velcroed to my boot. Pretty good, I thought. And until I dropped part of my sandwich on the floor the dog wearing the coat didn't even wake up.

Canine Sports Injury and Therapy

Wow! There's an impressive sounding heading for you. Now all I need is the three-volume set to go under the title! Actually, I have dogs to train this winter so I'll try to condense it down a little here for the sake of time.

The Iditarod veterinary program has a handbook on basic care of sled dogs regarding injuries and such, so you should probably look that over if you're thinking about the Iditarod.

Besides taking care of the feet as we have already discussed, most of the problems you will have with sore dogs will involve wrists and shoulders. Generally, the faster you go the more problems you will see with wrists and shoulders. Often you won't even know when or how the dog got sore but after a run you will notice him limping or favoring a limb. He may just have a muscle cramp or small bruise, so just because a dog is a little sore after a run doesn't mean he needs a lot of extra attention. For this reason, I like to wait at least an hour after a hard training run before I really check dogs over for injuries. It keeps me from worrying unnecessarily about every little cramp.

Check the wrists for soreness by bending the wrist back until the foot touches the back of the foreleg. Give a slight squeeze and watch the dog's reaction. If he cries out he is pretty sore. Many sore dogs won't say anything, but they will draw up slightly on the leg you are testing and extend their head forward, squinting their eyes in a body language message that says, "That hurts." Sore wrists will usually have some amount of swelling but it may not show up until the next day.

Older dogs may not have enough range of motion in their wrists to get the foot back to the leg so don't force it. If they don't seem sore don't let on to them they have a problem. Be sure you check the feet too, because if the dog has a bad foot and you squeeze it while checking the wrist, he may wince because of the foot and you could end up worrying about the wrong thing.

Shoulders should be tested for range of motion and soreness. Grab the front leg just below the elbow and with the lower leg folded up against the front of the upper leg, move it back and up until the upper leg is parallel with the dog's back, but no further. (You can make any dog "squeak" if you hyperextend a joint.)

Next, put your hand behind his elbow, and extend the front leg out straight in front of the dog until it is nearly parallel and in line with the dog's back. Watch the dog for any pain reaction.

Shoulders are a little trickier than wrists because flexing the shoulder could get you a reaction if the painful spot is anywhere from mid-spine to the head, and down to the elbow. You can find it if you practice and know what to look for but the most common sore muscles are the triceps and pectorals. These do respond fairly well to simple therapy but still take some time to heal.

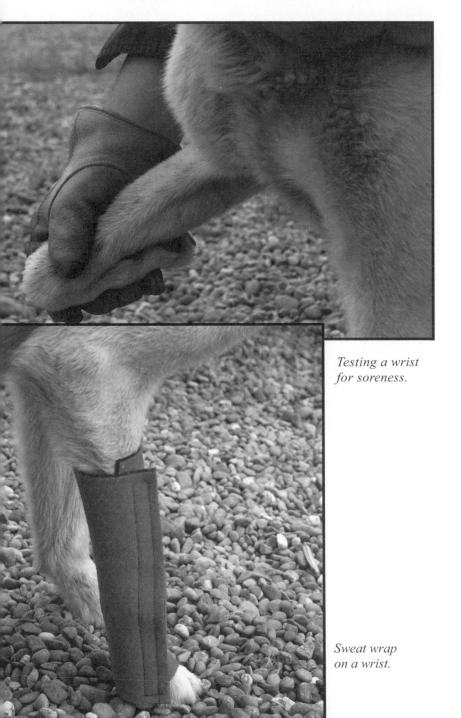

Testing a wrist for soreness.

Sweat wrap on a wrist.

Care and Feeding of the World's Best Athletes

Test a shoulder for soreness by flexing forward and back.

Check your dogs' feet, shoulders and wrists as a matter of routine, as these areas account for the majority of physical problems with sled dogs. Most of the time there will be no problems and you will get used to what they are like when normal so when a problem crops up you will spot it right away.

Another thing to be aware of is harness rub. Just inspect visually or by feel especially in the dogs "armpits." Poorly designed and poorly fitting harnesses will ride up into the armpit because of the angle at which the dog is pulling in these particular harness systems and can cause severe rubs if you don't notice it in time. You have to change harness style or size and put on a topical treatment to protect the area and promote healing. Time off will probably be necessary.

Okay, say you have a sore wrist on a dog an hour after the run. You rub it down with Algyval and put a neoprene wrist wrap on it. These are available from supply outfits. Put it on around the wrist, extending down so just the toes are sticking out. Make it fairly snug at the top and leave it looser the further down you go. The purpose of the wrap is to create a sweat and keep the heat in. It's not a compression wrap. Vets will tell you to cover the whole foot and the toes to prevent the toes from swelling, and that's okay when they're sitting on straw in a race, but at home when you are trying to keep these miserable things on a dog for a week they really don't like their feet covered or stepping on the wrap when they walk. They won't leave it on if you cover the foot.

Rub the wrist down every evening and put the wrap on. Cross your fingers and hope, or use athletic tape, whichever you feel will be most effective to keep the wrap on all night. Take the wrap off in the morning or rake up the little pieces from the dog's area and leave it off during the day. You don't want to immobilize the joint too much.

Leave this dog off from training completely for at least seven days, or two days after he seems to be pain free. On day eight or so, run him at a slow pace for four miles in a small team. If he doesn't get too sore run him eight miles on day nine, and 12 miles on day ten. Give him another day off and he should be able to rejoin the program on about day 12 for a 20-mile run. This is a best-case scenario here, so it may take more time off if the injury is worse or your dog is a wimp.

Occasionally, if there is quite a bit of swelling in the wrist when the injury is new I will put an ice pack on it for a while to knock the swelling down, and then go to the wrist wraps in about a half an hour.

For sore shoulders, rub the entire area down with Algyval or your favorite snake oil. Massage the muscles pretty good and put on a shoulder coat, also available from mushing supply places. These coats have pockets inside, to put chemical hand warmers in, on each shoulder over the triceps area and in the chest for pectorals. Put a fresh heater in every evening but leave the coat on as much as you can, day and night. Again, the dog will probably figure out how terribly entertaining it is to chew your cute little coat to shreds. You may have to keep him in the house or shop with you for a few hours a day so you can watch him and keep him distracted while the heat pack and coat do their magic.

For shoulders, leave the dog off for at least ten days, no exceptions. If you run him too soon you just re-injure or inflame the problem and set him back, almost to square one on healing. Just as bad, you teach the dog to think about the injury and you could really damage his confidence. "You mean I'm not invincible?"

Use the same gradual build up approach as for wrists; just give them a longer time off at first. After each of your build-up runs gently check to see if he's sore or not. A little soreness may be expected but a big setback means another week off.

Again, don't rush the healing process. Extra time off won't really hurt anything but running too much too soon means the dog may spend the rest of the season or longer on and off with rehab. You can usually adjust your training runs later to get the necessary miles on your rehab dog to get him back in the team. Remember, above all you want to get your best young dogs to the starting line.

I keep a spreadsheet on my computer, logging the mileage of all training runs and other pertinent information for each dog. The dates are across the top, and each dog's name down the side. Every run gets recorded for each dog. Pertinent notes about the dogs performance, heat cycles, and even the position in which they ran in the team can be recorded. Have your kids program the cells and rows to give you mileage totals monthly and year-to-date. You can use it as a planner as well, if you insert notes about future engagements or deadlines. Training milestones and benchmarks can be included to be sure you are on track with your goals. But one of the most important uses of the mileage chart is to record dates of injuries and therapy schedules. Be precise about your rehab regimen and keep track of the dates. This type of spreadsheet works well.

And one of my pet peeves: Don't keep testing the dog's shoulders all the time once you know he's injured. Every time you stretch that muscle to the point it makes the dog cry out, you may be re-tearing newly mended and tender tissue. This type of thing really gets my ulcer going during races. Now I admit I'm not known for promoting group hugs with race vets anyway. That's just not a part of my racing reputation that I have – how shall I say – culti-vated. But there are a few I highly respect and take their advice without question (almost). By the way, the ones I respect the most are also the ones who acknowledge that there is at least a slight possibility of the musher knowing a thing or two as well, and even (gasp!) something the vet may not know.

But here I come into a checkpoint with a dog in a shoulder coat, heat pack blazing in the left shoulder pocket and buzzards falling over 'cause of the smell of liniment all over the dog and filling the air. (Or were they super cubs?) "Your white wheel dog is limping," the rookie vet proclaims for the listening enjoyment of all of my competitors and every attentive citizen between here and Nova Scotia.

"Noooo, really?" says I, with only the utmost of respect in my voice.

While I'm stripping the booties off the team, Vet Lite takes the coat off my sore dog and proceeds to hyperextend my girl's shoulder until she screams. I charge the vet, and go for the throat. I would've got her too, if not for the huge boots on my feet and the other vet on duty who body slammed me into the snow bank. Okay, not exactly, but the scenario did play out in my mind. The second vet is one whom I highly respect and though she may be too small to body slam me, she straightened the whole situation out with a little reason, of all things.

To Vet Jr. she says, "See that shoulder coat? That's right, the one you took off the dog. Mm-hm. See the heat pack in the left pocket? Yes, that pocket. Very good. Now, do you smell that funny smell that is dropping ravens out of the sky? No it's not illegal, its liniment. Yes dear, I think this particular musher is probably aware of the problem with his dog.

"So there!" I added, still hopping up and down in place in my oversized boots.

"Now be a dear and just run along up to the cabin and put us on a cup of tea will you? I'll just finish up here."

You can often find the exact sore spot on a dog by lightly brushing your hand over the area, touching only the tips of the guard hairs. It's like an early warning system for the dog. If he is really relaxed, you can often see him pull back or quiver when your hand brushes over the sore spot. Another way you can find sore and inflamed spots is to feel with your hands for excessive heat in the area.

Occasionally I have had a dog I just gave up on for the rest of the season. He missed so much training through rehab time I thought he was out of it for the Iditarod. After forgetting about him on the back row for about six weeks I may find the ranks of the team a little thin and there's my dropout, with quite a bit of training on him, all fat and sassy and healthy as can be. These guys can come back in and run in a not-super-competitive team and do well if you get a few serious runs on them before the race. It makes me wonder why we don't do that with all of them sometimes.

This section obviously only brushes over the subject of injury and therapy and the longer you work with dogs the more tricks you will have up your sleeve. I suppose I could write a separate section of "farmer wisdom" on every part of a sled dog from teeth to tail, inside and out. This whole injury rehab issue is one of the most frustrating aspects of distance mushing. Often we run major races with one or more of our superstars at home nursing some boo-boo. Well, two things. Remember the 10 mph speed limit? If you aren't smart enough to keep the speed down when you should, you can hurt even your best dogs. In fact that's often what happens. And the second point is; if the son-of-a-gun who you call your best dog is hurt all the time, then he isn't actually your best dog at all, you just thought he was.

Eleven: Equipment

This is an area that some guys like more than others and I would put myself squarely in the same camp with "others." A lot of the stuff you see isn't going to help one sniff if you don't have the dog team to make it count. On the other hand I have seen plenty of situations where equipment failures or oversights have cost a lot of time. I have put considerable time into innovations that work for me, but the most important thing is to be comfortable with your gear and familiar enough with it so you can fix it when it breaks.

Those of us who have raced the Iditarod many times seem to face a dilemma of sorts. We are experienced enough to get by with minimal gear and experienced enough not to be caught without extra gear. Don't haul a bunch of junk you never use but a few extra ounces or even pounds for a repair kit, vet bag, spare dog food or cooker fuel can save your race sometimes.

Don't take anything more complicated than a pair of socks on a race without using it in training first. Practice with your stuff and be sure it works for you. Know how to fix things under primitive conditions. Anything you invented yourself had better be tested good and hard before you rely on it because if it is something you need, you will probably get the chance to fix it under primitive conditions.

I don't intend to major on equipment details here because that's the one area that is pretty well covered in other places. Websites, publications and periodicals are pretty good where information on mushing junk is concerned. Of course there are a lot of vendors more than willing to tell you all about it. You can see a lot of what is being used for yourself too, if you look in the right places. Besides that, seasoned mushers seem more than eager to tell you all about their latest inventions and clever ideas on equipment but start asking pointed questions about training or breeding for example, and the guys look like a Boy Scout troop being asked how the girly magazine made it into the tent. A lot of throat clearing and dirt kicking takes place.

Sleds

I have been building sleds since high school shop class, and I have them pretty well figured out. Of course I had them pretty well figured out when I built the "perfect" sled at age 14. It was a super lightweight wooden basket sled. The next year I built another "perfect" sled, a heavy bottomed toboggan sled. A couple of years later I built the "really perfect" sled which had a high basket about 10 inches off the ground. Later the "perfect" sled was a lower basket sled, then a raised toboggan. Later I lowered my raised sled, and raised my toboggan bed. Still later I made the "ultimate perfect" sled, a tunnel bed toboggan. Then along came Charlie Boulding's easy-rider sled, which, of course, I perfected. Still later was the Jeff King tail-dragger sled, which I pretty much copied except that unlike his, mine is the "all time perfect" sled.

One time I was broken down in Rainy Pass with a "perfect" sled whose only problem (among others) was two badly bent aluminum runners. Where there was once a perfect curve in the runners there was now an abrupt skyward kink, a souvenir of the Happy (ho-ho, hee-hee, ha-ha) River steps. The Happy River region of Alaska is home to a peculiar species of spruce tree which shows signs of aggression towards any other type of wood. For example, if one is driving a hickory sled in the Happy River region, the spruce tree may become distinctly aggressive, and may even jump in front of the invading wood species and smash it to smithereens. This same territorial behavior has been observed toward red oak, white oak, ash, birch and other types of wood. This is why dog drivers who are also knowledgeable woodsmen and familiar with the ways of Alaska's spruce trees increasingly rely on such non-wood materials as aluminum, fiberglass, polyethylene, Kevlar and carbon fiber for sled building.

Some people from "Outside" have lobbied for counseling or rehab for the trees, and until they show signs of improvement, complete avoidance of their habitat by intruders. Most hardcore, and some might say primitive or Barbaric, mushers would take a more direct approach. We want to solve the problem with a little chainsaw therapy, delicately administered of course. There are areas of the trail, however, where there are laws prohibiting this and any other method that would actually work, like bulldozers.

It is curious to some of us why preservation of these few "Individuals" out in the middle of nowhere is so important. I'm sure it isn't for their beauty because the only people who ever get within a country mile and have the opportunity to see them, don't actually see them at all because our eyes are shut tight in panic as we careen through the area.

I had limped my busted-up sled into the Rainy Pass checkpoint and promptly got on the radio to get my other sled shipped from McGrath. It was sort of a junker but it turned out to be "perfect" because it could be unbolted, broken down and wedged into a Cessna 180 aircraft. A fact I didn't remember designing into the sled when I built it, but in hindsight I'm sure it must have been done on purpose for just such an occasion. I got it reassembled and departed the checkpoint some two hours after I had hoped to leave. Regardless, I was "Happy" to have any kind of sled at all with two functional runners, a place to put my junk, a brake and something on the front to hook the dogs to. There were times during my extended stay, waiting for the plane to arrive, that I looked longingly at the large steel sleds being towed behind the snow machines at the lodge. I might have been able to hitch my team to one of those and drive it to Rohn. They are pretty tough. No wood to arouse the spruce trees. "Perfect" for the infamous Dalzell Gorge.

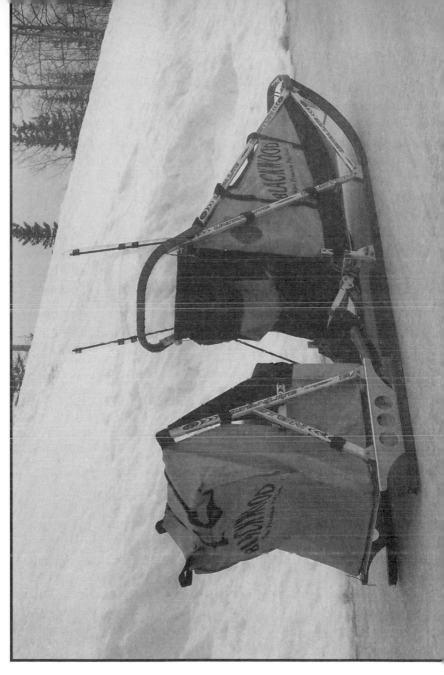

The perfect sled (so far)!

Towlines and Harnesses

For many years I have used a towline with spreaders between the tug lines to keep the tug lines parallel with the main line. The purpose is to do away with the inward angle pull on the dog's hips that "traditional" towlines cause. The dog runs straight forward, and all the force is straight ahead. All my dogs learn to run straight, stay on their own side, and put a lot on that tug line. Many a dog gets credit for being a good puller in the angle-pull towlines when actually he is leaning out against the tug line and not really pulling forward very much. Get an engineer or physicist to explain what that does for your forward progress, or take it from me– not very much.

My necklines are bungee-core poly and stretch to 30". Add snaps, collar slack or whatever and the dogs can get six feet apart if they need to. That's plenty of room in my mind, so I don't see that as a reason to abandon necklines completely. However, I won't hesitate to unhook it on a particular dog for a few runs if the bum finds some use for it that I don't appreciate, like too much snow biting or getting a tow. Again, they have to be forward oriented, with or without a neckline.

In the past several years I have developed a harness much like the freight harnesses of the past, only much more streamlined. They have a small spreader behind the tail, and two elastic straps, which keep the webbing off the dog's hips entirely and allow a straight line of pull from the shoulders to the sled. They completely eliminate any pressure on the dog's hips and back and compliment the straight-line pull concept of the spreader towline.

Some of my more fashion-conscious competitors don't like the spreaders. They just don't look cool. What can I say? Draft animals from alpacas to horses the world over, for tens of thousands of years, have been hitched to

Equipment

loads with a harness system much like mine. I feel the harness and towline system should be anatomically correct even if the dog isn't pulling as much as an ox. It makes a difference over the long haul. People have said the system just looks more complex. Fair enough, but I feel a certain amount of complexity is necessary for a properly function-ing system. Taking simplicity to an extreme, you could just hook them up by the collar I suppose, but we all know that wouldn't be the best.

Windsor modeling a correctly fitting harness.
I wonder what Robin is telling him!

A team working in an ideal spreader-type towline,
everyone pulling straight ahead.
Well, there's one in every crowd, I guess.

Equipment

Snow hooks

Snow hooks are the curved, sharp pointed, double pronged "anchors" used to secure a dog team for stops along the trail in the winter. They come in many shapes and sizes, most of which will work well under ideal hooking conditions such as hard packed snow, but you want one that works on glare ice, too. I carry two on the sled at all times, one ice/snow hook, and one lightweight aluminum snow hook. You need to be able to hook a tree, so I don't really care for the ones with extra fins included in their anatomy that get in the way for tree hooking.

I use my ice/snow hook for most stops and the lightweight aluminum hook to hold the front of the team when camping. I keep them both rigged to the towline while traveling so I can use both hooks to hold the team when they are fired up and I'm worried about holding them with just one hook. I also like to leave a tail on my snow hook rope so when I hook a tree I can use the extra rope to tie a safety loop in case the hook falls off the tree.

So once you have two good hooks on your sled you're all set, just remember the cardinal rule of snow hooks: Don't ever trust a snow hook. Never, ever go behind your hooks.

As I found out a couple of winters ago, never, ever go on your hooks either. I'll explain.

I was almost home at the end of a long and very cold run, but man, did I ever need to drain the bilges. Well, I just couldn't make it home. So, much as I hated to at these temperatures, I decided to stop and take care of business. Since it was near the end of the run I thought one hook would hold them, but being cautious nonetheless, I stood on that hook to be sure it stayed put. Well, the lame-brains weren't as settled down as I thought and just as I was getting things worked out there, between polypropylene underwear, fleece pants, snow pants and wind gear, and trying to take aim between the bottom of my parka, dangling mitten strings, headlight cord and a sheath knife, they gave a pretty good jerk and popped that hook out, with me standing on it. It had the effect of yanking my feet right out from under me. Down I went and off they went before I even went!

Nowadays I always walk at least part way up beside the team to perform this particular function in case they do it again. I refuse to turn my back on 'em too, so it leads to some awkward situations with curious dogs, especially if the trail isn't too wide. Oh well, they're only dogs. At least this way I have a chance to grab the sled as it goes by if I need to, and jump on. But if they do take off before I'm done, I'm not sure how I will do everything needing to be done at that particular point in time, with only two hands!

Firearms

Many years ago, my son Danny and I met Iditarod veteran Tim Osmar and his handler George at Tim's cabin in the Caribou Hills. We were going on a run up to Caribou Lake, once Tim and George rebuilt their towlines that is. Danny, twelve at the time, got frustrated watching George fumble with the lines and finished the task for him. Tim was almost done too, when George experienced a rare moment of lucidity, and reported that there were tons of moose near Caribou Lake, and asked if anyone had a gun along. Tim spoke up first, so I saw no immediate reason to announce what I was carrying.

"Yeah, I've got a gun in the sled," Tim answered, and went back to his fid and lines. George looked satisfied and relieved, since he for some reason, perhaps legal in nature, didn't own a gun.

Equipment

"I don't have any bullets, though," Tim added, winking in Danny's direction. George looked confused, but that wasn't really unusual. Whatever he tried to say next probably wasn't in English, or any other language for that matter.

"We're set," Danny told Tim. He nodded.

So what do we need guns for? Nope, it wasn't hunting season, not for moose anyway. Around here when the snow gets deep the moose get ornery. They don't want to get off of the trail into the deep snow. They are hungry. They are tired of packs of canines attempting to eat them. They aren't in a good mood. So along comes a dog team and sometimes they aren't very nice.

It is my conviction that anyone who spends a lot of time in the out-of-doors, especially in the northern wilderness areas, really should carry a gun. Now if you are all by yourself and you don't want to carry a gun, then go ahead. Knock yourself out, as they say. Get eaten or stomped all by yourself. It's up to you.

But if you are responsible for anyone else's safety out there, you ought to be ready to defend them. This goes without saying where family and friends are concerned but what about dogs? They would do just fine on their own but in a team they are obviously restrained and can't even run away from danger. Simply put, their safety is entirely in your hands.

Now, if you are opposed to guns for some reason maybe you should choose a little tamer environment, or get over it.

Get a .44 magnum or larger and learn how to use it. Get some instruction and bang up about a dozen boxes of ammo until you can actually hit something. Get good with the doggone gun, you hear me? Don't be afraid of it, don't try to save on ammo, and don't be lazy. Shoot it until you are proficient and confident.

Actually hitting a charging target under stressful conditions is another matter, but I can't hold your hand here.

I do know, on pretty good authority, that moose will charge your headlamp in the dark and won't hesitate to stomp dogs and mushers. Bears (when not hibernating) will attack dogs, even in a yard of over 150. And wolves will sneak between the big dogs in the yard and yank the younger ones right out of their collars and eat them.

Carry the gun on your person when you are driving dogs, not in the sled. If you get knocked off your sled by a moose you will need to be able to get your gun. I am not making this up either.

One very cold night a crazy young bull moose charged my son Danny and his friends Caleb Banse and Jim Gallea as they mushed, each with their own team, on the gas pipeline about 20 miles from our place. The moose head-butted both Caleb and Danny, sending each airborne and began stomping around in their dog teams. Caleb tried to get back to his sled to retrieve his gun, and in so doing, provoked the moose to attack him again. As Caleb tried to flee, Danny made it back to his sled and got his gun. He was able to shoot the beast just as it ran his friend down. Caleb received only minor injuries and no doubt was spared a severe thrashing or worse from the 1200-pound animal.

That episode turned out okay, but we learned to keep the guns on our person at all times.

I am aware of mushers who have had to kill moose, brown bear, black bear, and wolves in defense of life and property (DLP), specifically themselves and their dogs. If it was the case that it had been myself who was involved in those situations I bet I could spin up a doozy of a story to go with each one. I'm just not sure what the statute of limitations is on game violations. Actually, DLP kills are legal in Alaska but you're supposed to report it. Cops

Equipment

and paperwork are two things some Alaskans just don't go much out of their way to get involved with.

Personal Gear

This sport requires a lot of stuff to wear. I'm not going to try to tell you exactly how to dress because you won't listen anyway. Everyone ends up with a set of gear that they like or else what they got for free or cheap somewhere. I'll just give you a few observations.

I like to use a lot of layers so you have flexibility to take off or put on clothes depending on the weather. There's no sense messing around with anything other than synthetics that are light and retain their warmth even when wet. I grew up in this sport in the era of cotton, wool and down, and it has taken me decades to get over a very real phobia of my gear getting wet. To this day I often spend too much time at checkpoints drying my gear, forgetting that it is 90% as warm wet as it is dry.

I learned a lot about synthetic insulated gear in my first Iditarod race in 1982. I was ready to go from the starting line with good gear for those days, mostly insulated with goose down. My parka, storm pants and sleeping bag were down for sure. My sister worked for a sporting goods store at the time and showed up just before the start with a couple of things she had talked the store manager out of as a sponsorship for me. She had a fleece jacket, a Holo-fill vest, and a Polarguard sleeping bag, all new fangled synthetic gear. Even back then I knew the rule about not taking new stuff on a race but the consequences of that mistake surely would be minor compared to telling my sister that I didn't appreciate the new gear she had gotten me. So I tossed out my old reliable super-duper "Siberian Penguin" down bag and put in her little phony-fill bag or whatever-the-heck it was. She wanted to see the jacket and vest on me, so I obliged. What else could I do? I had to go in 36 minutes, so I didn't have nearly enough time to try to talk her out of it.

Well, I never took that jacket off until I got to Nome, and the vest was too hot so I kept it for a spare. And the sleeping bag may have saved my life.

I spent nearly 48 hours between Unalakleet and Shaktoolik that year in a doozy of a storm. A good share of the time it was blowing hard and a white out, and the snow blew into my clothes like flour. That fine coastal snow seems to be able to get through the tightest weave nylon fabric, and zippers seem to be an open door. I walked for many hours leading my dogs and got pretty hot, so between the blowing snow and perspiration I was soaking wet, even with the temperature not far over zero. Finally, in an era before reflective trail markers, darkness and low visibility forced me to stop, only about six miles from Shaktoolik.

Now I ought to just go on and whip up one jaw-dropper of a tale here about the storm and 60 mile-per-hour winds and me as a rookie being missing and reported lost, running out of food, water, and fuel, about the frostbite to my hands and all, and how I led the dogs through the storm on foot for hours. But heck, if it's all true, storytelling isn't half as much fun, and besides, this section is supposed to be about gear and clothing and such.

So it gets dark and I decide to call it a day, so I just tie off to the last spruce pole marker I could find and pull all the dogs around the downwind side of the sled into a big pile. Then I start to rearrange my sled so there is room for me to get inside. As I pull out my tarp, the wind catches it and yanks it right out of my grip, and it takes off for Siberia like some crazy bat-ghost-thing. Then I try to get my sleeping bag open in some way so I can climb in, and as I hold the top in my right hand the wind grabs that too. Like a giant wind sock at the airport that bag jerked out tight

Equipment

to the west, and came oh-so-sickeningly-close to taking off after the lost tarp. I got hold of it with both hands and managed to get it in the sled and myself in the bag and the sled bag closed up. I don't even like to think about what would have happened to me if the wind had gotten that bag away from me.

Even as I curled up in that synthetic bag inside the sled, I felt the snow blowing through the fabric of the sled bag, in my face and into the sleeping bag. "You could get in trouble here," my numb brain tried to tell me. "You are going to get really cold." With the last of my energy I sat up as best I could and dug out that Holofill vest and put it on over my fleece jacket. I put the down parka back on too, though it was soaked and not much good. I fell asleep as soon as I lay back down, the wind still screeching outside my sled bag cocoon.

When I woke up the wind had dropped down to about 25 mph and it was getting light out. I tried to sit up, but I was stuck fast. The wind had blown all night and had forced drifted snow into every nook and cranny of the inside of that sled. The entire sled bag was packed tight, inside and out. The inside of the sleeping bag was wet and steaming, and outside the snow was packed hard and frozen like a rock. The down parka I was still wearing was soaking wet and flat as a pancake, like two layers of nylon with little lumps here and there where the poofy down was supposed to be. My down storm pants were in about the same shape.

I'm pretty sure, given the condition of my down pants and parka, that if I had been relying on a down sleeping bag rather than that phony-fill one from my sister, I probably wouldn't have woken up that morning. I was pretty close to hypothermia when I crawled in and I don't think I would have made it if I had gotten much colder. Now I wasn't toasty warm, mind you, but I made it through with the synthetic jacket, vest, and sleeping bag.

I eventually got out of the sled and on the trail to Shaktoolik. I arrived there not long after Joe Redington, Sr. who reported having a night a lot like mine. He had been pretty worried about me I guess, and expressed as much relief at seeing me straggle into Shaktoolik as if I had been his own kid or something.

Boots

Okay, I have finally figured it out.

Have you ever wondered how boot manufacturers test their products to give them a temperature rating? For example, the Snow Monster boot from Blue Heel Boot Company is rated for something like 185 below zero. No, really. Okay, maybe it's only 135 below. What's the difference? There is no place on the face of the earth that gets 135 below, and I'll bet you a week's pay the pretty-boy modeling the boots in the catalogue would never set foot there anyway.

So I called the manufacturer and they say they flew to Greenland to test their boots and the ratings are real. So now I get it. You see, the only time I ever heard of 135 below I was at cruising altitude in a jet aircraft.

So two of the guys from the catalogue are sitting in first class drinking martinis on their way from Chicago to Amsterdam and the pilot comes on and says they are flying over Greenland at 40,000 feet and the temperature is 135 below outside the cockpit.

"Tony, how are your feet?"

"My what?"

"Your feet. We're testing the Snow Monster, remember?"

"Oh you're a snow monster, silly! I completely spaced that out, so I'm wearing sandals, but I did remember to put on my socks."

Equipment

"Well, I'm wearing the Snow Monsters, and it's 135 below out, we're over Greenland, and my feet are roasty-toasty."

So if you ever wondered how they rate boots, I'm pretty sure that's it. It has nothing whatsoever to do with actual outdoorsmen wearing boots under actual conditions in the cold on the actual face of the earth. The ones rated to minus 40 may work for doing chores in the winter at zero if you hurry, but boots that are good for 135 below? C'mon.

In cold weather, I wear insulated custom-made mukluks with a hard rubber sole, and felt liners and insoles inside. This works out for me because our kennel manager used to be a shoe maker. I suggest you try the Northern Outfitters boots or Wiggy's insulated mukluks over running or hiking shoes. Whatever you wear, you will need a hard sole to stomp on brake bars and snow hooks. Soft mukluks like traditional fur boots and Steger mukluks leave my tootsies feeling pretty vulnerable to getting smashed. Pack boots featuring rubber up over the top of the foot are guaranteed to retain moisture and get cold after a few hours even if they are rated to 135 below.

Twelve:
What's Between Your Ears?

Mushing's Dirty Little Secret

Every sport has one I suppose. A dirty secret I mean. Something the folks close to the sport are ashamed of. Cycling has performance enhancing drugs. Baseball has illegal betting. Snowboarding has performance inhibiting drugs. Horse racing has horses. Mushing is no different.

The image of a distance musher is a rugged one, promoted by the mushers themselves, the media, and well, promoters. Mushers are tough, impervious to pain, and able to cope in a harsh environment. They expect the same from their dogs. Yes, mushers are tough as nails. So what would you expect?

So here goes: Mushers are pretty much big softies.

There, I said it. The secret is out. Mushers may be tough on the outside but on the inside they are just… mush. At least where their dogs are concerned.

I have seen a six-footer with ice in his mustache shed real tears over an injured dog. I have seen an Iditarod champion (5' 6") kiss, yes actually kiss a dog on the nose. That could be "dirty". Another champion I know is "prone" to sleep on the straw with his dogs (though sometimes he sits up). That could be "dirty" too. Mushers rub their dogs' feet, talk to them like babies, call them cutesy little nick names, and worry about their stools (feces) like a new mother examining the contents of a diaper. That is definitely "dirty". Race veterinarians patiently examine every dog at every checkpoint and often go over certain dogs again at the request of the musher.

"Pee Wee may have had a slight limp about 20 miles back. It was only for a few steps and I'm not sure, but he stopped to take a wee pee and he hobbled a little I think, maybe, so if you could just look at him again. I think it was on the left side but it could have been the right..."

Not everyone is like that of course. Take me for example. I am tough on the outside and tough clear through. No mush here. Every dog better pull his weight or that's it for him. (Now, don't go quoting me out of context here. This is sarcasm, for those of you who used to be a politician, are a politician, or want to be a politician in the future, have ever demonstrated for any cause or if you donate to more than two registered charities. And lawyers.) There, that should just about cover anyone I haven't previously offended.

It was a snowy, windy day in November. Cold, as I recall. We were working in the shop, and along about noon a smallish, blackish dog with curly-ish hair waddles slowly into the yard. He looked and acted like he was about 20 years old. "Must be one of the neighbors dogs," says I, though I had never seen him before. One of the boys put him on the four-wheeler and took him the half-mile to the corner near the neighbor's house and dropped him off, thinking he would go home.

Well it was near dark, so about four hours later, this little beggar comes slow-poking it back into the yard. I reckon it took him the whole four hours to make it back from the neighbor's. I saw him out the window but since I was either busy on a project or arguing politics with one of the handlers I didn't go out right away. About half an hour later I see the dog sitting all cute-like in the bag of a dog sled out in front of the shop. When I called him he ignored me because he was deaf, but when he saw me he tried to come but he just couldn't make it out of the sled bag. Poor little cuss. Homeless, tired, and so crippled he couldn't even climb eight inches out of a dog sled.

Turns out he was crippled all right but that wasn't why he couldn't come to me. He must have climbed in the sled to get out of the wind but the Velcro on the sled bag had taken a liking to his "poodlish" hair and wasn't about to let go. He was stuck, overcome by the Curse of the Velcro. Just one of many good reasons why poodle-types shouldn't be long distance sled dogs.

So I had to help him out and as I did I discovered this dog was covered with lumps all over his body. Probably cancer. He was in rough shape. We brought him in, called the neighbors who had never seen him before, and kept him until he died in the spring. He was house broken, didn't eat much, wagged his tail a lot, never complained, and stayed out of the way. "Bentley" we called him.

The little cuss was probably abandoned and needed a place to spend his last days so he chose us. Twice. There were a few damp eyes around the place that morning we found him dead. Of course not me, I mean the female handler and my wife and such. Well, I guess I liked him a little, too. He kept sawdust from collecting in a small spot in the corner of the shop floor.

Attitude

So now, if you've done everything I've told you and haven't messed it up too bad, if you've resisted the urge to try every dang-fool idea that popped into your head, at least until you have checked it out with someone who knows, and if you've put a lot of work and even more money into it, you may have a half-decent touring team by now. It's not as good as you think it is but maybe half-decent.

Now you think you are ready to race. I've already laid my wager that you won't be patient enough to just travel with your team on their first long distance race. You will be thinking, "In spite of that stupid rag I read by that Seavey dude, I know quite a bit about this and I seem to have a natural gift. And when I saw Annie Beavertail out on the Mukluk Trail, from the smile on her face I'm sure she thinks I'm a top twenty team. And if Annie likes my team then it must be something special."

Forget about it. Annie probably just noticed the fifteen-foot toilet paper streamer coming out the back of your Army surplus snow pants. That explains the smile. Anyway, Annie, like a lot of your top mushers, may just have a soft spot for fools who try the same path they have already stumbled down. Don't mistake a little encouragement or a sympathy compliment as a stamp of approval from a top driver.

You need to maintain a humble and realistic attitude regarding the ability of your team and yourself. Not only will this keep you from being humiliated (so badly anyway), it will cause you to be fair to your team and run them according to their actual abilities, rather than your inflated self image.

"Entitlement-itis"

"One has to learn how to run before walking 'round breathing that millionaire." - Jimmy Buffett

Well, this next bit isn't really written for you. Nope, it's written for some other less noble person who may have slipped through our extensive screening process and got hold of this book somehow. You probably want to just skip the next three or four paragraphs because surely they don't apply to you anyway.

You (actually the "other guy") have put a whole year or two into this dog team (whoopty-doo) and spent two whole summers wages from working at Subway or Home Depot (wow) and you have trained and trained (at least half as much as Seavey recommends). So you think "They" owe you the chance to run the Iditarod, the Last Great Race on Earth. "They" include potential sponsors, Iditarod champions, the board of directors, race staff, race sponsors, volunteers, village elders, feed stores, credit card companies, institutions of higher learning, your parents, girlfriend, children, dogs, moose and anyone else with a pulse and an I.Q. higher than yours!

Not only do you think "They" owe it to you, you think "They" ought to thank you for the opportunity to provide you with the opportunity to race, including a free ride home when you fail miserably and quit half way through! After all, with the current champions getting older, you are the future of the race, right? Well, I've got news for you Princess, I for one am not certifying anyone as the future of the race until they have a little past to go with it. And with that kind of attitude you aren't likely to be the future of anything as difficult as running the Iditarod or other long distance sled dog race.

Get back here; I'm not finished with you yet!

If that's a pretty accurate description of your thinking then I have a pit out back of my dog yard with plenty of room for your attitude. It will blend right in.

If you run across that "other guy" with that kind of attitude you tell him for me that a race is just that, a race. A contest. It isn't an entitlement. It isn't food stamps, either. Nobody owes you any tiny little part of anything it takes to do this. You aren't entitled to even run dogs unless you can afford it, let alone start a race, much less finish. Every little bit of it you have to earn and work for and then get used to spending many an off-season with the ache of disappointment as your closest companion. It's just plain tough from the first twinkle in your eye until your knees and back give out decades later.

Some of the newer guys will be the great champions of the future, no doubt. But they will stand on a podium of mushing tradition thousands of years deep, and hoist trophies polished with the sweat and tears of at least a generation of racing pioneers who have broken trail for them.

Listen, this attitude of entitlement is a blight on our sport, and a source of great embarrassment to some of us. It seems that even people who haven't yet put together a dog team, let alone an informed perspective, feel entitled to bash mushers, volunteers, race organizations, and especially decision-makers, like boards of directors. Any sport should have spirited debate and fan involvement, but it gets out of hand in mushing. Yes, as mushers we are independent thinkers and must overcome long odds to succeed. We often buck the establishment in many ways; indeed we must, to survive in this sport. Let's not confuse "bucking the Man" with biting the hand that feeds us.

I may not be the sharpest tool in the shed but I'm pretty sure these newbie mushers or non-mushers aren't the most qualified people in the whole wide world to make decisions for race organizations. Helpful and well thought-out suggestions are always well received, but a lot of the comments I hear are neither helpful nor well thought-out. They border on lunacy. No volunteer or employee of a race organization deserves to be slandered, lied about, verbally abused, or threatened, either through gossip, confrontation, or on Internet forums. Yet a lot of people who have no clue, other than they may know someone with dogs or they may want to run the Iditarod some day, are doing just that.

Besides being annoying and embarrassing, here's the real problem: a sizeable portion of the public in general is wary of our sport on some level. Most that bother to look into it are usually satisfied that it is a healthy and wholesome activity for all involved. But we do have critics. When mushers rage on like lunatics, either in public or on discussion forums, they raise doubts as to just what kind of human beings we are.

Conduct yourself in a mature, professional, humble and dignified manner at all times if you get involved in our sport and expect to overcome staggering odds to more than earn anything you may ever get out of this crazy-person's game.

Epilogue

Well, so there you have it from a guy who has been running dogs for over 40 years. As some of you have probably guessed, I can go on about dogs just about forever. To some of you it probably seems like I already have.

I have been sitting here trying to figure out why I have spent umpty-nine hours over a span of a couple of years pecking away at a keyboard, knowing all the while that it will likely benefit me very little, and in fact, probably give me more than one headache before all is said and done. What the heck was I thinking?

I guess it's sort of like most people getting started in sled dogs. You start out with a couple of dogs and before you know it you have a whole yard full. Now, what do I do with a whole yard full of dogs? Well, if I had just a few more I could race. Same with this book. It started out with a few notes for our own handlers and puppy team drivers. Then if I added a little I could hand it out to others, and then, well, if it was more complete I could pass it off as a book, at least among friends in the mushing world. Shoot, I'm even making mental notes for later in case I want to write something about actually running your first Iditarod Race.

I have had the honor of running dogs almost all my life, starting at four years old in 1963, and since 1992 my family has derived virtually all of our income from dog mushing through our tour business and racing. At that time we had just returned to Alaska from living Outside for a few years, and we were dead broke. So broke in fact, we barely limped into my parents' yard with a broken down van and an even more broken down utility trailer. My wife and I had three young boys and not much else to our names, and at 33 years old I moved back in with my parents for over a year. If not for Mom and Dad we would have been living in the van.

We got a few dogs from my dad and a few for cheap and free here and there and started our tour business. My wife Janine, though not actually a musher at all, conducted kennel tours and gamely fielded questions as best she could. After hours she kept the books, promoted the business, and attended to a million other details you would never associate with sled dogs. She kept house, and raised and home schooled the boys. Our older sons Danny, Tyrell, and Dallas (ages five to ten at the time) were our only crew and handlers for the first several years. By age twelve these boys were doing a man-sized day's work and never even knew complaining was an option.

Through good fortune and hard work, and "a little help from my friends," we have done okay for ourselves since then. I owe most of my humble success to my loyal family, the great Alaskan Husky and elbow grease.

I had run my first Iditarod earlier, in 1982, and got back into racing in 1994 when I ran the Copper Basin 300 for the first of many times. I ran the Iditarod again in 1995, and have run it every year since.

I may be one of the lucky few that have made a life out of this sport, but I don't think it is all luck, and I can promise you it isn't easy. Nobody knocks down your door trying to give you anything.

Epilogue

On the other hand, I have had the privilege of becoming intimately acquainted with the most amazing animal on the planet. I have had the privilege of running dogs through the arctic wilderness where few people get to travel. I have had the privilege of participating many times in the Iditarod, the Last Great Race on Earth. Most of all, I have had the privilege of doing all of this with my dad and later with my own sons. I am blessed.

So, I guess I am coming around to the real answer to my earlier question. Why am I writing this? I kind of wanted to pass on a little of what I have been honored to do for four decades, so far. If it helps out a few folks of honest heart and open mind, who want to learn about sled dogs, well, I'm willing to share my perspective.

Most importantly, I hope those just starting out in the sport of dog mushing will one day experience that special relationship with a fine team of sled dogs and the absolute joy of traveling with them through the frozen wilderness.

Lead, Follow or Get Out of the Way!